Praise for **SQUIRCLE**

"At a historical time when probably more than ever we need to rethink the way we think, SQUIRCLE offers a fresh sustainable path forward and a decisive business competitive advantage."

CAROLINE BROWN, MANAGING DIRECTOR,
INVESTMENT FIRM CLOSED LOOP PARTNERS, NEW YORK CITY, NY

"SQUIRCLE infuses the power of nature back into modern life. Once you discover this practical and profound tool, it will quickly become your guiding force."

DEBORAH BURNS, FORMER CHIEF INNOVATION OFFICER,
HACHETTE MEDIA, NEW YORK CITY, NY

"SQUIRCLE is the book for those of us who suspected logical analysis may not provide all the solutions in life. In his new book, Cholle offers a refreshingly simple concept for a more comprehensive approach: If we allow our intuition, gut feelings and emotions to inform our decision-making, we will arrive at novel answers to many problems that we had tackled for a long time. This holistic jump will catapult us to the next level of understanding the world around us. SQUIRCLE is not just a thought-provoking resource and a workbook for business teams; it is a must-read for physicians, for scientists and for leaders in all fields."

MATTHIAS STELZNER, MD, FACS, PROFESSOR OF SURGERY &
DEPARTMENT CHAIR, UNIVERSITY OF CALIFORNIA AT LOS ANGELES/VA,
GREATER LOS ANGELES, CA

"My career started in media and I work today in entertainment. Both industries keep being disrupted. Personal reinvention is daily routine. From first-hand experience SQUIRCLE is both fun and effective and made a radical difference in the way I now adapt to change."

PHILIPPE GUELTON, PRESIDENT AND HEAD OF VOD NETWORKS, CRACKLE PLUS TV AND CHICKEN SOUP FOR THE SOUL ENTERTAINMENT, NEW YORK CITY, NY

"When I first discovered SQUIRCLE, I immediately thought: 'This is what women business owners need today'"

HILARY LENTINI, CALIFORNIA WOMEN'S LEADERSHIP EXPERT. FOUNDER AND CREATIVE DIRECTOR, LENTINI DESIGN & MARKETING, LOS ANGELES, CA

"My direct reports and I worked with Cholle. We all embraced a SQUIRCLE mindset. I saw my team of finance and IT executives transform in front of my eyes over a two-day offsite."

OLIVIER LEONETTI, CHIEF FINANCIAL OFFICER & TECHNOLOGY OFFICER, ZEBRA TECHNOLOGIES, CHICAGO, IL

"It's as simple as it gets, yet quite truthfully mind-blowing. Square gives us structure. Circle gives us energy. Today we need both probably more than ever"

FLORENCE DEPREZ-WRIGHT, AUTHOR, TV PRODUCER, LOS ANGELES, CA

"For Olympic Games athletes, to reach peak performance demands strenuous training, but in the end, it is all about the right mindset. Before, during and after the competition, to bring mind and body into synergy makes a world of difference to reach the top of the podium."

CARLOS LAMADRID, DIRECTOR OF DEVELOPMENT, US SKI AND SNOWBOARD FOUNDATION, PARK CITY, UTAH

"I relish in Cholle's ability to turn inside out the way we approach life. Everyone needs to read this book. SQUIRCLE is brilliant!"

BARBARA STEHLÉ, PHD. ART HISTORIAN, FOUNDER, ART INTELLIGENTSIA, JERSEY CITY, NJ

"When we stop to consider that half the class of 2030 will be in occupations that have not yet been conceptualized, solving problems that have hitherto not been articulated, it strikes me that the most successful employees of the future will implicitly embody the SQUIRCLE way of thinking."

MICHAEL MANISKA, HEAD OF SCHOOL, INTERNATIONAL SCHOOL OF LOS ANGELES – LILA, LOS ANGELES, CA

"A very astute take on profoundly important new insights. It's all kind of genius. Bravo!"

NATACHA POLAERT, FOUNDER AND DIRECTOR, OFF PARADISE, CONTEMPORARY ART GALLERY, NEW YORK CITY, NY

"Cholle is a master communicator whose SQUIRCLE model, techniques and tools for expanding creativity in order to find innovative solutions to problems can help everyone, no matter what field they're in."

DANIEL MILDER, DIRECTOR AND PRODUCER, JERSEY CITY, NJ

SQUIRCLE

A NEW WAY TO THINK
FOR A NEW WORLD

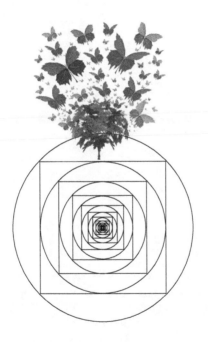

*Embrace your natural ability
to live in uncertainty and thrive
in an age of possibilities*

A la que sabe.

Nature doesn't hurry,
yet everything is
accomplished.

LAO TZU

contents

author's note

"The physical world is real." That is supposed to be
the fundamental hypothesis. . . It appears to me
that the "real" is an intrinsically empty, meaningless
category (pigeonhole), whose monstrous importance
lies only in the fact that I can do certain things in it and
not certain others.[1]

—ALBERT EINSTEIN

It's not about peace on earth,
but about peace with Earth.

—TIOKASIN GHOSTHORSE,
2016 NOBEL PEACE PRIZE NOMINEE

W hen I was a young child, an unsettling dream kept visiting me. An anonymous voice would repeatedly tell me that my dream world was reality and that my daily life was illusory. I would awaken, bewildered by this reversal, and struggle to determine which realm was my actual life. The dream also had a language all its own that my family, all of whom were scientists by trade, could not translate. This language, I realized later in life, was as different from regular language as my mind was from theirs. The dream eventually left me as I got older, disappearing behind a veil of unresolved feelings.

Since then, I have always been drawn to the mysterious, to what is hidden underneath or alongside. I have examined and turned the pages of my life, striving to understand myself and my place in the world. After receiving a master's degree in the science of management, more unconventional paths have stretched me and brought peace: art publishing in Paris, theater and opera in New York, yoga in India, even a degree in clinical psychology. All have shaped my personal take on life and provided me with insights into human nature, as well as a concern for the sustainability of the modern world and the need to reexamine the way we think.

When I sit on a beach, I enjoy being in a vast, expansive space and seeing the horizon far away and an open sky above. Intuitions abound when pensive, alone in nature. One day, looking at Santa Monica Bay from a beach north of the Malibu pier, I could not fathom what I was seeing as a plane crossing the sky caught my eye. A menacing, brownish-gray cloud of pollution was suspended over the shoreline. In a flash, I saw just how the human mind, which had been capable of engineering and perfecting even a way to fly, could also recklessly disregard nature. Modern prosperity has been made possible largely by the powerful forces of science, but without our realizing it, the scientific mindset of rigor, predictability, and careful experimentation has translated into a culture of dominance and control designed to combat our fear of nature and stifle its unpredictability. In the name of progress, we approach life in linear ways. We have disconnected from the parts of ourselves that are not about rationality, including our sensations, emotions, and deeper perceptions. We tamp down the natural instincts that are essential for us to thrive, just as they are for every other creature on the planet. Suddenly and profoundly, I was absolutely certain that feelings and intuition were every bit as important for positive, sustainable decision-making as discipline and rigor. A vision for a new way to balance body and mind, being and doing, instinct and rationality was born within me. Only later did I realize that this deeper understanding of reality was in fact the calling given me in my childhood dream. SQUIRCLE does not intend to label these opposing tendencies as good or bad or to put anyone in one category or another. Obviously each one of us is more complex than this simple model, and we all evolve as we go through life. As you become familiar with SQUIRCLE, you will be able to see for yourself that it is both easy to understand and of deep impact to your personal and professional life. It is designed to trigger inner reflection and introspective conversations with others so that we can engage with the deeper part of ourselves and make decisions that result in better personal outcomes and a better future for all.

At this time of unprecedented crisis and undeniable unknown, it is more important than ever to challenge the assumptions that we base our decisions upon as we create our individual and collective reality, one decision at a time. The current crisis shines light on the power of nature in our lives in a way that is unescapable. It is calling us to take heed and rethink, adapt, and transform the way we live. It seems clear that the time has come to place nature back at the center of our worldview. This will have to start at an individual level and require us all to recognize that nature is our best teacher and that we need an intimate understanding of it to become fully human. SQUIRCLE is the tool to help you do just that. This book invites you to pause and be open to its lessons. I hope that you enjoy the journey.

We need to link our minds
to our hearts and use
our native knowledge,
science and innovative
technologies wisely to
make better decisions
about people, animals and
our shared planet.[2]

— JANE GOODALL

introduction

The supreme task of the physicist is to arrive at those universal elementary laws from which the cosmos can be built up by pure deduction. There is no logical path to these laws; only intuition, resting on sympathetic understanding of experience, can reach them.[1]

— ALBERT EINSTEIN

No, no. You're not thinking! You're just being logical.

— NIELS BOHR, 1927 NOBEL PRIZE IN PHYSICS

Have you ever experienced a deep feeling of injustice? Or felt slapped in the face because you were considered incapable of achieving something based on preconceived notions about your age, gender, ethnic background, sexual orientation, or physical limitations? Before you even had a chance to try to prove that you could do it?

Meet Virginie Delalande. When she was nine months old, medical tests revealed that she could hear no noise lower than the roar of a plane taking off. Doctors concluded that she was born deaf. At school, she couldn't be taught how to speak. She was told that she could not become a veterinary doctor, which was her childhood dream.

Later in life, she was also told that, despite her burning desire to represent and defend the rights of people in compromised situations, being a lawyer would not be possible for her. Yet today, she's a vibrant, positive, magnetic, and voluble woman who lives a rich life. She gives public talks in French, her mother tongue, using her own voice to eloquently share her journey of learning to speak and becoming a lawyer. She had big hurdles to overcome, to say the least.

Whereas the United States and much of northern Europe recognize the capacity of deaf people to be professionals in almost any field, France is behind in this regard. If you are born French and deaf, you were once doomed to be silent, but this doesn't have to be the case, as proven by Virginie, who taught herself to lip-read.

She then taught herself to speak and today communicates with a voice she has never heard herself. She is the first deaf French female lawyer. Those who tried to convince Virginie that she would never be able to use her voice in this way no doubt believed their words were justified by reason and norms, yet in reality, by relying solely on an obtuse and fixed logic, these narrow-minded individuals cut the fragile wings off the butterfly before it escaped its chrysalis, even though it had the means to do so. Instead of encouraging it to fly, they suppressed its confidence and potential, relegating it to the role of caterpillar forever. Virginie could have become a prisoner of their confined and limited thinking, but ultimately, she was able to transcend it. It takes an enormous amount of character to break out of these logical shackles.

Once, Virginie and I were both part of the roster of speakers at a conference. The night before the event started, we were invited to dinner by the owners of the vineyard and spa resort where the conference was held. Virginie's peaceful and beaming presence was noticeable, but I would have never been able to guess what she was about to share onstage two days later.

After Virginie had told her poignant and compelling story, she was asked by one attendee whether, if she were given the opportunity to hear, she would welcome it. Her answer came without any hesitation whatsoever: "No." She explained that being deaf had actually made her an incredible listener and highly perceptive person. When she enters a room, she is able to sense people's moods and interpersonal dynamics. She picks up on cues and nuances that others usually don't notice. It helps her a great deal in life, both at work and at home.

Virginie's story teaches us two essential lessons that are at the heart of what SQUIRCLE stands for. First, it shows us that most of us live life as if we were listening to two different radio programs at once. One is comprised of our rational thinking based on logical deduction and induction. The other is our subjective appreciation of life based on emotions and feelings. Obviously both channels bring value to our lives. The French doctors who advised Virginie in her youth believed, according to their evidence-based medical knowledge, that there was no way for her to ever be able to speak, but Virginie's own subjective inner knowing and intuition told her that it was possible. Had she listened solely to the objective radio program, Virginie would have gone on to lead a very different life, but the other, more subjective program made her intuitively feel that she knew differently, or knew better, than what she was told. And she did. Life validated her inner knowing. Clearly, what felt true to Virginie was unique to her, and the path that she chose is not a formula for success for every person born with a hearing impairment. But what's true for all of us is that we have the freedom to make informed decisions that honor our inner feelings and deeper aspirations, even if they don't initially make sense or fit within the norms of society. In fact, sometimes this is the wiser route.

Second, over the course of her unique journey to learn to speak, Virginie opened herself up to another level of perception, a level of sensitivity that has enriched her life so much that she would not give it up even to hear. For those of us who were born with normal hearing abilities, it might be hard to believe that someone born deaf would ever turn down the offer to recover their sense of hearing. But Virginie did so, even though she does not know from firsthand experience what it is like to hear. From observing others, she is convinced that she perceives the world in a way that is richer and more multifaceted, a way that is, she believes, better than simply hearing.

This is what SQUIRCLE is humbly trying to help you do: honor your inner knowing in a world that all too often relies on hard facts and logic to the point that it limits humans' natural capacity for creative adaptation, and to expand your sensitivity and perceptiveness beyond what we think is normal or possible so that you can deal with the complexity of today's world. SQUIRCLE offers this in a straightforward and simple way that transcends individual cultures and belief systems and can be explained and experienced even by a five-year-old.

SQUIRCLE is an adaptation of a science-based model that I developed for executives and organizations based on years of research on the creative culture of L'Oréal, a world leader in the beauty industry, and on managerial practices in a variety of industries of all sizes on five continents. This model has helped more than two hundred and fifty thousand Fortune 500 executives as well as students at prestigious business schools, including Wharton and Columbia. It is a revolutionary mindset that you can adopt in everyday life, at home or at work, for your personal and shared benefit. It requires no preexisting knowledge on your part. You simply have to find and integrate the innate intelligence, power, creativity, agility, and resilience that naturally lie within you.

"Not long ago, people thought of emotions as old stuff, as just feelings—feelings that had little to do with rational decision-making, or got in the way of it," António Damásio, professor of neuroscience and director of the Brain and Creativity Institute at the University of Southern California says. "Now that position has reversed. We understand emotions as practical action programs that work to solve a problem, often before we're conscious of it. These processes are at work continually, in pilots, leaders of expeditions, parents, all of us." [2]

Dr. Gerd Gigerenzer of the Max Planck Institute for Human Development in Berlin explains in his book *Risk Savvy: How to Make Good Decisions* [3] that it would be erroneous to assume that intelligence is necessarily conscious and deliberate. We know more than we can tell. There is in our guts an undeniable capacity for helping us make intelligent choices among complex data. We all have an enormous opportunity to make use of these additional problem-solving skills and harness our powers for complex decision-making. Doing so requires only a change in attitude, the same way that Virginie Delalande found the courage to embrace uncharted possibilities and be open to experimentation.

I call this mindset the SQUIRCLE Attitude, and it offers a new way to engage in situations and adapt to them.

The inspiration for SQUIRCLE was born at the beginning of the millennium when I asked myself, How is it that human beings are able to travel to the moon and yet are unable to sustain a balanced relationship with nature? Looking up to that plane and the brown cloud above Santa Monica Bay, I wondered, What is the root cause of this split in the human mind?

I began to imagine an answer to this question: if only we could include nature (intuition and instinct) in our thought processes and decisions, chances are we would design solutions that are inevitably more respectful of nature. To prove that this type of holistic decision-making could help both people and businesses better adapt, innovate, and succeed, I started a consulting practice, The Human Company. We have since been hired and rehired by the CEOs of some of the most successful global companies because our unique methodology has brought them unprecedented transformation and success.

Today we all exist with levels of disruption and uncertainty that we have not experienced since the Second World War, to the point that leadership experts and the US Army College introduced the notion of a VUCA world, where the acronym stands for Volatile, Uncertain, Complex, and Ambiguous, to describe and reflect today's instability. Global conflicts, pandemics, climate change, the rise of artificial intelligence, and rapidly shifting business and political landscapes have combined to make constant adaptation the new normal.

But adapting is not always easy; it requires personal change. Transitions are hard and intimidating, and it takes courage to step into the unknown. Resistance kicks in, and we often revert to established patterns or regressive behaviors. This is the moment when SQUIRCLE can make a difference.

As such, this book is designed for:

- All individuals across generations and demographics who have strong instincts or gut feelings about situations or decisions but cannot always articulate why they do, or effectively advocate for their ideas;

- Anyone who wants to learn how to tap into their natural intuition and creativity and make better use of them in their everyday life;

- Any professional who knows deep inside that they need to reinvent their skill set to succeed in an uncertain environment where the old way is no longer working;

- Anyone who aspires to rebalance our modern way of living with a greater respect for nature;

- All people who understand that changing the world starts within.

Last but not least, this book was written with women in mind—and all men who care about them. Research by the renowned consulting firm McKinsey shows that women offer a different approach and attitude in situations, both in business and beyond, that can provide unique, direct solutions to problems and even to our cultural entanglements. Yet the same research also showed that women feel their contributions are often neglected, if not negated.

The fact is that women have the keys to the type of leadership of which we will need more and more in the future.[4] A 2016 study in the *Harvard Business Review* showed that women boost performance and innovation in organizations. Women display collaborative and holistic behaviors that men can emulate, and their natural ability to make complex decisions makes them better board directors.[5]

A study conducted by bestselling authors John Gerzema and Michael D'Antonio for their book *The Athena Doctrine* showed that among sixty-four thousand people surveyed in thirteen nations, 63 percent of men said that the world would be a better place if men thought more like women.

Even if progress is happening in certain areas, it is still very slow. We need to help women advance more quickly and be in a better position to influence our culture. At a conference for the World Economic Forum in August 2019, Melinda Gates reminded the audience that it would take 208 years to close the gender gap globally if current trends persist.[6]

For too long we have been talking about men and women, masculine and feminine, with certain expectations about traits that are associated with each and often opposed to one another, such as mind and body, linear and nonlinear thinking, the rational and the emotional, active and passive, planning and improvising, control and surrender, and doing and being. This gendering of our culture makes us defensive. Judgmental. Resistant. We need to stop polarizing and start recognizing that these seemingly opposing approaches, as seen in Virginie Delalande's story, are all necessary to life, complementary, and already living inside of us.

With SQUIRCLE, in order to move beyond stereotypes, these sets of traits are known by two different, genderless, and universal words: SQUARE and CIRCLE. SQUIRCLE—that is, SQUARE and CIRCLE coming together in a novel way—frees us from polarity to better embrace nature and the complexity, creativity and agility that lie within us in order to regain our inborn capacity for adaptation.

The time has come to bring systemic change across societies and generations, and SQUIRCLE holds the key. This promising adventure starts with each one of us.

A New Way to Perform Better (With Less Effort)

Intelligence is the ability to adapt to change.

— STEPHEN HAWKING

Move with the flow. Don't fight the current. Resist nothing. Let life carry you. Don't try to carry it.

— OPRAH WINFREY

"This is incredible! This game is just like a life-changing experience I had a couple of years ago!" Philipp said. Like the other participants in my seminar, Philipp had just played the SQUIRCLE Game, an exercise The Human Company does with our corporate clients to help them develop the ability to succeed in today's disruptive environment. The game shows participants how to naturally access their untapped potential to adapt and collaborate with those around them, both increasingly important skills in a fast-changing world.

We were almost done debriefing when Philipp spoke up to share his story. Philipp was in his midforties and looked very fit.

He told us that he enjoyed running and had completed many marathons over the years.

A couple of years prior, he had decided to run the New York City Marathon for a second time. As usual, he said, he started preparing over the summer, three months before the event. The first two months, he did a great job of keeping up with his training regimen, but in the third month, it had become challenging for him to stay on track because of travel for work. He found it almost impossible to train during the last week before the marathon.

Two days before the race, he woke up with doubts about whether he should run at all. He called his coach, Jennifer, for advice. Jennifer listened to him quietly and waited a few seconds after Philipp had finished speaking. Then she said, "If you're afraid of hurting yourself because you're not at the top of your game, I would say there's no real need to worry. You've trained intensively for the past two months, and when you started your routine you were already in very good shape overall. A few weeks are not enough to wipe away the good work you've consistently done over the years. Your body is used to running marathons. Safety is not an issue here. But if you are hesitating because you're worried about how well you're going to perform, I would recommend the following: for dinner, eat your special fitness meal that you usually eat the day before the race. And, obviously, get a good night's sleep."

She then shared some additional advice that for Philipp was quite unusual. She said, "I recommend for your own sake and for your growth as an athlete that you experiment with a new approach during the race. First, never look at your watch. Second, stay connected to your breathing. I want you to follow this advice throughout the entire marathon. I know that this might sound strange, and I'm sure that for a highly competitive man like you it must be hard to even imagine how you could run for hours without ever evaluating mileage against time and only paying attention to your breath. But my recommendation is to try something different. Since you don't feel at the top of your capacity anyway, you might as well give it a shot and see what happens."

Philipp hung up, fairly stunned by what he had heard. Jennifer was a demanding coach with a strong focus on discipline and routine when it came to training, diet, and sleep. Over the years, she had gotten Philipp used to carefully monitoring charts about every aspect of his training process. He had been expecting a conversation more about data and analytics than about breathing and ignoring his watch. The whole thing felt a bit "touchy-feely" to him. He wasn't sure what to make of it. He decided to go to bed and reevaluate the situation in the morning.

Over breakfast the next day, he thought about his conversation with Jennifer. The words that kept popping into his mind were *You might as well try something new and see what you get.* Unexpectedly, for someone like him, who typically sought control over his life in order to achieve his goals no matter what, these words resonated. He felt Jennifer had a point. "After all," he thought, "I've come this far, maybe I'll get something out of it." He decided to follow her advice.

By then, everyone in the room—including me—was eager to hear the end of Philipp's story. He explained to us that even though it had not been at all easy for him at first, he managed to both not look at his watch and stay connected to his breathing. In fact, focusing on his breath actually helped him feel less anxious about his pace and keep his eyes away from his watch. As it turned out, this unusual way of monitoring himself and his progress during a marathon enabled him to score his best time ever!

Why Philipp succeeded

Despite the fact that we generally take breathing for granted, we know from science that short, sharp breath is related to the nervous system's fight-or-flight response and can actually induce feelings of stress.[1] When we are stressed, we are less likely to make responsible choices or do our best. Yoga demonstrates this clearly. Experienced yoga teachers make the poses look effortless and often quite beautiful, but the practice itself is physically demanding. Without proper breathing, students can struggle and become more susceptible to injuries. If you ask experienced practitioners how they manage to flow so gracefully through the postures, they will tell you that it is because they are deeply connected to their breathing.

When I share this story during retreats or seminars, I often hear similar testimonials. Amalia, a business school student, was a competitive swimmer in high school and trained every day. One race day, a rush of adrenaline took her by surprise right before she dove into the water, and she became overwhelmed and confused. In a split second, as she began her strokes, she decided to surrender to her body and her breathing. She recalls that this was the only decision that made sense to her in the moment. She lost track of time and of everything else in her environment as she propelled herself forward. She achieved her best time ever.

Another one of my students, Quentin, told a similar story. He had run a half marathon two different times. The first time, he ran with the fear of not being fast enough, and while completing the race, he badly injured his knees, which required significant recuperation. The second time, he decided to run just to enjoy the experience for what it was, a fun run on a beautiful day. He had a great time, no injury, and even beat the goal he had set for himself by one second!

Jump into the unknown and let go of the outcome

The reason I bring up these athletic examples is that they have a useful common denominator: two different ways of going about the same experience. One way is about carefully analyzing and planning in order to secure an outcome. Initially, Philipp wanted a sure strategy to avoid physical injury and reach his best score. The other way is about experimenting with new possibilities to discover new outcomes, a jump into the unknown that involves connecting to sensations and feelings as much as to data and knowledge and that involves relaxing and letting go as opposed to pushing hard. In all these stories, the second approach proved to have powerful results.

There is another striking commonality. Surprisingly, when our protagonists let go of the outcome, they reach their *best* performance. This defies conventional wisdom. They didn't reach their goal through a meticulously planned strategy; instead, they chose another route. They improvised, experimented, became very present, and surrendered to the process with no preconceived notions or even a clear understanding of how it would unfold. Through more openness and less control, they all achieved more with less effort.

Why is it that we often keep pushing and forcing our way through life when we don't have to? Why do we feel the need to be in charge, to manipulate outcomes and our environment, and to always follow the rules? What if we could find a way to do better and accomplish more with greater ease by breaking free of the constraints that circumscribe our thinking and actions? In the next chapter, this cultural bias will be explained. As you discover SQUIRCLE in the chapters that follow, you will see how it can help us shift away from this pervasive inclination to resort to coercive force and toward the many other creative options that are available. SQUIRCLE will enable you to make space for a whole new realm of possibilities and personal resources that will allow you to reach new heights.

QUESTIONS

- Do you remember a time when you were open to experimentation and let go of your need for a certain outcome?
- If yes, why did you decide to do so? How did it feel?
- If no, would you be willing to give it a try next time? How do you feel when you think about doing so?

The Square
Mindset

> When you look at the bigger picture, [. . .] you
> realize that either you change and adapt, or, as
> a species, you go extinct.
>
> —LOUISE LEAKEY

> Language for me narrates the pictures in my mind.
>
> —TEMPLE GRANDIN

One day in San Francisco, at a leadership seminar for
a Fortune 500 company, I told participants the story
of Philipp, our marathon runner in the previous
chapter. One senior executive was skeptical of the idea that we
can organically and even spontaneously adapt to reach higher
levels of physical performance with little effort. At one point she
told me, "Francis, we all know that there are many factors that
can affect the performance of a marathon runner, from what he
eats the night before to weather conditions or even simply the
gear he chooses to wear. So how do we know for sure that it was
Philipp's change of approach that catalyzed his increase in speed
and time?"

I thanked her for her terrific question because it gave me an opportunity to make an important point. Obviously, the answer is that there is no way to know except through experience, and any experience involving oneself will always include some subjective observations as well as objective ones. That's the painful fact. As a result, you will not know if it is possible until you yourself adopt Philipp's approach, experiment with familiar situations in new ways, and evaluate the outcomes based on your own perceptions and feelings as well as on data and hard facts. This is the journey of any scientific researcher. One of France's greatest mathematicians and theoretical physicists, Henri Poincaré, who was also a philosopher of science, famously said, "It is by logic that we prove but by intuition that we discover. To know how to criticize is good but to know how to create is better."[1] Scientific research is clearly a discovery process, and your experience with SQUIRCLE will be the same. It may take some trial and error, but if you let your natural intuition guide you alongside reasoning, you will find the answers and achieve the results that you seek— and they will likely be better than expected.

In their book **Super Thinking,** _MIT graduates and coauthors Gabriel Weinberg and Dr. Lauren McCann define the scientific method as "a rigorous cycle of making observations, formulating hypotheses, testing them, analyzing data, and developing new theories." The cycle they describe starts with observations, which require_

But the question I often hear is, "Francis, can we really trust our perceptions and feelings to make a reliable judgment call?" This concern is understandable. My answer comes in the form of another question: *"Can you afford to not notice your perceptions and feelings to make a reliable judgment call, especially when so many of our decisions involve other living beings?"*

To explore these questions, let's play a simple and short game together. You will need to get a piece of paper and a pen or pencil. Take a deep breath, relax, and try to get out of your head and connect with your body. Now look around you.

First, notice the squares, rectangular shapes, straight lines, and angles that appear everywhere you look. How do they make you feel? Write down the words that come into your mind. No overthinking, no censorship, no second-guessing. Let the words crossing your mind land on your page.

either a perceptual process (using the observer's subjective senses) or a nonperceptual process (using objective machines or theories) or both. Therefore, allowing subjective impressions, feelings, and inclinations to affect your process is not only permissible—it's often essential.

Now take another deep breath, relax, and connect with your body. Look around once more. This time, spot the curves, circles, and oval shapes that you see. How do they make you feel? Notice the sensations in your body. Again, write down all the words that enter your mind.

Now look at what you wrote. Chances are that your list about straight lines, angles, and rectangles includes words like *order, efficient, reliable, rigid, distant, confined,* and your list about curves, circles, and ovals includes words like *creative, adaptable, welcoming, inclusive, fluid, warm,* or comparable words. Over the years, I have asked thousands of people around the world with different backgrounds and professions to do this simple exercise. We always end up with two very distinct groups of words and with very homogeneous words in each group.

The first group is about order, predictability, reliability, and linearity. Let's represent it with a Square.

The other is about fluidity, creativity, infinity, and inclusiveness. Let's associate it with a Circle.

Now, let's expand on the meaning of Square and Circle and on how they reflect our reality and how we think.

The Square symbolizes an approach that is rational and logical. To illustrate the concept of Square, think of taking a multiple-choice exam. Your answers will be either right or wrong, and either you will answer enough questions correctly to pass or you will fail. Consider a game like chess, in which every move you can make on the chessboard is clearly defined by set rules. Or think of a stop sign on the road, which represents a message without any ambiguity: you have to bring your car to a standstill. It's a fixed process with a black-and-white outcome.

The Circle symbolizes an approach that is fluid and intuitive. To make the Circle explicit, let's take the example of skiing downhill. When you ski, you need to constantly adjust to the terrain, visibility, and quality of snow. Your process is unpredictable and in flux. You have to go with the flow and constantly improvise. Here is another example: hiring a nanny for your child. You will have to not only do background checks and ask applicants specific questions and process their answers carefully, you will also undoubtedly pay attention to their body language and how you feel about their overall demeanor and personality. You rely on a set of questions, but also on something more. The discovery process is open-ended and could go any number of ways. The outcome will not always be black and white.

In life, we obviously need both Square and Circle approaches and their complementary qualities. We have to be punctual to hold meetings and meet deadlines. We have to approach going to the airport with a Square mindset in order to be on time, bring the correct luggage, and be at the right gate. On the other hand, it is unthinkable that our lives be governed by a schedule and rules at all times. We need spontaneity and improvisation to connect with our families, relax, and enjoy life. The same goes for food. We know we need to eat according to certain principles, but we also need to be able to make choices in the moment based on sensations and feelings.

In some instances, it's clearly better to approach living life with a Circle mindset, in others with a Square mindset. We should honor both as their balance shifts through the day. Sometimes we need to be careful about time: when we need to leave on time for a job interview, we need to look at our watch. And sometimes it's not so important: when we decide to stay home and chill, we can forget about the clock. Sometimes it's a matter of survival to be connected to our senses—to smell smoke and escape a dangerous fire, for instance. And sometimes it's not useful to be in touch with our feelings, such as when we add numbers to create an expense report.

Square and Circle Qualities

SQUARE

Accurate – Decisive – Capable – Competent – Detailed – Diligent – Efficient – Logical – Mature – Neat – Practical – Prudent – Rational – Realistic – Sensible – Good planner Concerned with numbers – Time sensitive – Budget conscious – Cautious with risk – Comfortable with the familiar

CIRCLE

Adaptable – Comfortable – Emotional – Open – Independent Informal – Inventive – Original – Playful – Intuitive – Resilient Romantic – Spiritual – Unique – Versatile – Seeking new or better – Quickly bored – Shorter attention span/loses focus easily – Easily amused – Dreamer – Artistic – Creative thinker

---

What's important is to become more aware of these respective qualities without any limiting judgment. One approach, the Square, is good because it is formulaic. Like the stop sign or algebra, it is unambiguous and dependable. The other, the Circle, is organic, and therefore more difficult to engage because it cannot be turned into a formula. Like improvising on the keyboard or getting to know someone, it requires our presence and attention. Unfortunately, we live in a society that values one over the other. **As a culture, we tend to love what makes sense and have negative prejudice toward what's not logical.** When making decisions, we often realize that our feelings can be of help, but we question their reliability. We believe that hunches can be useful, but we're also quick to scrutinize them and to wonder whether we can really trust them. We all want to make the best decisions in life. We want to gather facts, understand the situation rationally, and recall similar past experiences in order to avoid repeating mistakes. For really important decisions, we want to be aware of our personal cognitive biases so that they don't cloud our judgment. We may want to honor our values and feelings, but our culture is much more comfortable with the dependability of Square.

Often the result is that in the name of logic, we become illogical. We try to make our feelings and hunches fit into a formula; we want them to be fully dependable, and when they don't fit, we think we should dismiss them. But feelings and hunches are not formulaic. Wanting absolute clarity and dependability from them is exactly like wishing for ideal weather all the time and expecting to have a handy switch to control it at will. It's clearly impossible, yet that's the unreasonable and unaware approach that we apply to almost every aspect of our lives.

How can people and organizations thrive in disruption? When the Square becomes dominant it belittles the Circle and deprives us of essential adaptive and problem-solving skills. This is probably one of our biggest cognitive biases, yet I rarely see it discussed. In my advisory work with CEOs, I meet strong, driven leaders with exceptional analytical skills, strategic capacities, and often rare intuitive abilities. Yet in their organizations, complex problems and team collaboration are approached in a Square dominant way more often than not. Once the CEOs recognize this and its side effects on their business, their mindset shifts and in turn, this impacts their organizations. This is the defining factor that allowed billion-dollar companies to succeed at reinventing themselves and overcome daunting business challenges, when recommendations of even the best strategic management consulting firms had not been enough to bring forth the level of transformation needed by our clients. Becoming aware of the dominance of the Square is the pivotal process that naturally unleashes an untapped innate potential in everyone. That is key to adapting and thriving in disruption. For those eager to read about social proof of results, they can find it by flipping forward to chapter 11, and to the About the Author section for business cases and metrics.

Here is how this dominant mindset is best represented:

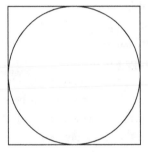

The Circle is only welcome if it fits inside the Square.

In other words, feelings, sensations, and creative ideas are only acceptable when they make sense. Otherwise, when they don't fit a Square framework, we're fast to dismiss them. That's a deep-seated habit in all of us.

When we were in primary school, we were taught letters and figures, and then, later on, we learned how to write and calculate. Without a doubt, all these skills are necessary to function in life. But these are conventions that are part of our culture, whereas our physical sensations and raw emotions are inborn and part of our nature. In fact, they are directly gifted to us *by* nature. It is obvious that by definition, our human conventions will never be able to match the complexity and diversity of the natural world, both inside and outside of us.

Even doctors seemingly most based in medical science know that being a physician requires them to listen, observe, and empathize with the patient to get to a deeper level of information about their health as a whole, beyond mere facts and lab results, yet from our earliest school years, we have been largely graded on our ability to reason, memorize, and analyze facts. We are taught to understand ourselves and life more through theories, frameworks, and knowledge procured by others than through physical, firsthand experiences like sports, drama, musical improvisation, or direct observation of nature. These activities are usually seen as ways to let off steam, exercise, and balance intellectual tasks like math, physics, or history. They clearly come second and are viewed as less important to our personal development and success in life. As adults, our work performance is most often evaluated based on metrics and the rules of the competitive marketplace, and we may be judged and employed based solely on numbers and our ability to generate profit. All this is to say that we very much tend to look at the world through the lens of the Square. As stated before, Square is a great tool: it is analytical, reliable, efficient, and productive, but it can also easily become dominant.

Emma and the Parrot

One day Emma noticed a nest with a parrot in her backyard. She kept looking at the bird, in awe of its beauty. Suddenly it took off and Emma lost sight of it. She was so mesmerized by this unexpected encounter that she decided to come back the next day, hoping to see it again, but when she returned the next morning, the parrot was not there. Emma kept coming back day after day, but the bird was never in its nest. One day, by chance, as she was walking in her backyard, she happened to see the parrot again. She was so happy, and she realized that she'd like to find a way to protect and keep the bird close to her. She began thinking of ways to do this. She imagined that she could replace its nest in the tree with a cage filled with food. This way, the parrot would go inside the cage and Emma could lock the door. She then imagined that she would give the parrot plenty of food and water every day. She would no longer need to worry about not seeing her new friend; the bird would always be there for her.

The problem is that a cage is not the same as a nest. In a cage, the parrot is fed and protected from predators, but it also loses its freedom and, bit by bit, its natural ability to survive in the wilderness. In a nest, the parrot is free and naturally adapts to its shifting environment. In a cage, it is dependent on others for its survival and becomes an object of decoration.

Now, think of the CIRCLE as this beautiful, green parrot and the

SQUARE as its cage, where the wild animal is no longer free to come and go, to soar, or to travel as far and wide as it likes. When you cage the CIRCLE inside the SQUARE, you are limited to the space of the cage, to what you know and to existing solutions. When you "free" the CIRCLE from the SQUARE inside of you, you are free to think, feel, and move in new, even radical directions, like the parrot leveraging its innate ability to create, adapt, be self-sustaining, and seek repose in a protective nest when that is necessary.

In general, science, language, and education are our nest. They are necessary and useful tools, but they should never become a cage to our natural abilities.

The problem with this cultural bias is that, when "Squared in," the qualities of the Circle—like creativity, fluidity, inclusivity—are clipped like the wings of a caged bird. But today, we as a society are in a constantly shifting and evolving environment where the old rules no longer apply, and we need to be innovative and adaptive to lead in the future. We've never needed our Circle abilities more than now! So how can we undo this prevailing bias toward the Square, as we use it for its best qualities, yet keep it from dominating the Circle? To start answering this question, in the next chapter we will further explore the controversial relationship between Square and Circle in modern life.

Throughout the book I mention "nature" and use the same word to designate three concepts that are intricately intertwined.

• "Nature in us": our body, our five senses, our intuition, our instinct, which all translate into sensations, emotions, gut feelings, perceptions, pain, pleasure...

• "Nature outside of us": plants, animals, forests, rivers, mountains, stones, rocks, air, wind, clouds, oceans...

• "Nature as in life": the creative process that unfolds in and around us, and keeps everything together in an order that eludes us all, even the greatest minds.

We, humans, are part of "nature outside of us". And as such, we're constantly influencing it and depending on it. "Nature in us" and "nature outside of us" are clearly interdependent to the point that they are inseparable and, in more ways than not, simply one and the same.

QUESTIONS

- What situations have you been in today that required a Square attitude? A Circle attitude?
- Have there been times when you have expressed your thoughts or opinions only to have them rejected because they were not fact driven? How did you feel when this happened?

03

Square vs. Circle: A Controversial Relationship

> Few are those who see with their own eyes
> and feel with their own hearts.
>
> —ALBERT EINSTEIN

> A mind is so closely shaped by the body and
> destined to serve it that only one mind could possibly
> arise in it. No body, never mind.
>
> —ANTÓNIO DAMÁSIO

Reason—or what we represent by Square—knows what's right and what's wrong, what's taller and what's shorter, what's rational and what's irrational. Square organizes everything in terms of opposites. It is an incredible tool for discrimination and evaluation, but we all know that nature is not binary. Nature is complex. People are complex. Life is complex. If in doubt, just ask scientific researchers, judges, and jurors. Or ask yourself about your current or past romantic relationships: Were they always clear-cut and easy to understand?

Let's take the opposites *rational* versus *irrational*, for instance. We've learned that two plus two equals four. We know that in the summer, plants in the garden need more water. We know that the more people there are in an elevator, the more weight the elevator will have to lift. All of these are rational statements. On the flip side, deciding to never go to bed or to stop sleeping altogether in order to have more time in the day for your passion projects or to improve your revenue is irrational. We know that if we never slept, we would end up in the hospital with severe, if not lethal, symptoms. Flying like a bird in the air might seem fascinating to some of us, but jumping off a cliff will not allow us to fly freely for long.

We all know what's rational and what's irrational. The logical mind can differentiate one from the other. But there's more to us and to life than these two options. Life is not only about these opposites, rational versus irrational. We tend to leave out the part of life that's complex. There is also what is *nonrational*, and this represents a category of its own.

where the problem starts

we look at the world as black & white

RATIONAL	IRRATIONAL
follows logic	doesn't follow logic
2+2=4	"If I don't sleep,
3<4	I will be healthier"

Now let's talk about Circle. Think of sensations, emotions, inspirations, perceptions, intuitions, and aspirations. There is no such thing as a rational or an irrational emotion. We might or might not enjoy feeling a particular emotion such as surprise, but regardless of whether we like it, it just is what it is: surprise. **An emotion is an instinctive response to what's happening in our life.** To feel cold on a hot summer day when most people feel hot is unusual, but it's not rational or irrational. The fact that this feeling is atypical does not automatically make it wrong or untrue. Instead, it is part of the category that we call *nonrational* and represent with a Circle.

what we're leaving out

the world has colors and nuances

RATIONAL	NON-RATIONAL	IRRATIONAL
follows logic	follows another logic	doesn't follow logic
2+2=4	"feelings, emotions,	"If I don't sleep,
3<4	perceptions, intuitions."	I will be healthier"

The challenge with this category is that it's hard to make sense of what's nonrational: how we feel, what inspires us, why motivation comes and goes, and so forth. It's even harder to measure. In a world where we've been taught from our earliest years to reason, analyze, and measure outcomes, it demands a real effort to stay in tune with the nonrational part of ourselves. It requires even more effort to understand it, utilize it, or simply express it.

For example, we use a relatively limited vocabulary to talk about emotions. We have essentially one word in English, *love*, to express a feeling that's vital to everyone's balance and fulfillment in life. Add a few more like *adore, cherish, worship, idolize, treasure, prize, dote on,* and *hold dear,* as well as phrases like *infatuated with, smitten with, besotted with, passionate about, devoted to, care very much for, feel deep affection for, think the world of,* and some informal ones like *mad, crazy, nuts, wild about* or *carry a torch for,* and you have twenty-two words and expressions altogether for this deep emotion. In contrast, the Sami people, who live in the northern tips of Scandinavia and Russia, have at least 180 words related to snow and ice.[1] This demonstrates just how much more nuance and diversity is possible within a single idea or concept.

Our culture lacks subtlety in vocabulary when it comes to this nonrational part of ourselves and of life. Equally serious, if not more so, is the fact that we equate what's nonrational with irrationality. When we make decisions about situations that are complex, we believe that paying attention to our emotions makes us irrational or less rational about our decision-making process. Why do we believe this? Because we apply a Square approach to our decision-making. We want to be sure that our process is fully reliable and will optimally produce the best outcome, but the Square is often the wrong lens to look through in a complex situation.

the mistake we make

we assimilate non-rational to irrational

RATIONAL	NON-RATIONAL	IRRATIONAL
follows logic	follows another logic	doesn't follow logic
2+2=4	"feelings, emotions,	"If I don't sleep,
3<4	perceptions, intuitions."	I will be healthier"

Applying the wrong lens takes away our natural capacity for sensing and appreciating nuances, as well as our propensity for creative thinking. Consequently, our process lacks depth. Neuroscience professor António Damásio, who teaches at the University of Southern California, has shown through functional neuroimaging that emotions play a central role in the way we process social interactions and decision-making.[2] Paying attention to our emotions, therefore, improves our ability to seize immediate opportunities to satiate our basic needs and ensure our survival. It also enhances our ability for future planning, as nature provides us with more nuanced data that we can analyze and build upon when looking ahead. Taking stock of our emotions does not guarantee that we'll make perfect decisions, but it is a sure way to open ourselves to new perspectives that can propel us to entirely fresh solutions. In today's unpredictable, rapidly changing world, **it is time for all of us to question the dominance of the Square over the Circle.** The irony is that even as we turn away from feeling and emotion, the business world is embracing them in order to build deeper relationships with their customers. Some Artificial Intelligence (AI) systems acknowledge emotions and factor them into their decision-making processes in order to sell to or serve their clients more efficiently.[3] But how can we do this for ourselves when the controlling Square approach is so prevailing and deeply rooted?

As we have seen, the human mind can typically be represented by a Squared-in Circle as in the image below.

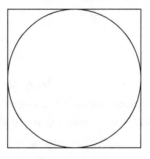

By definition, the Square is controlling. That is its essence. It develops strategies to secure outcomes. If you let the Square run the show, it will dominate the Circle. But what if we freed the Circle from the Square? What would happen? Will the Circle come to dominate the Square, or can they create a type of synergy? This is what we will explore in chapter 4.

QUESTIONS

- Do you remember a time when you made decisions based on Square norms rather than Circle personal feelings? How did you feel at the time? In hindsight, what were the consequences?
- Do you know people who are able to honor a Circle approach, even when it's hard to justify their actions and decisions because very few facts are available? How do you feel about these people and their actions? How often do you feel connected to your intuition? How does it feel when it happens?

04

Meet SQUIRCLE.
You Will Never
Forget It!

Sometimes surrender means giving up trying
to understand and becoming comfortable with
not knowing.

— ECKHART TOLLE

Don't let anyone rob you of your imagination, your
creativity, or your curiosity. It's your place in the world;
it's your life. Go on and do all you can with it, and
make it the life you want to live.

— MAE C. JEMISON

I n the previous chapter we saw the price that our culture pays for its prevailing Square bias: an inability to think outside the box and make decisions that address the depth and breadth of complex situations. This inability produces linear outcomes when transformative, game-changing solutions are needed. We see this manifested in the difficulties that businesses have with innovation; that education has with evolution; and that governments have with solving inequalities, environmental imbalances, and other problems. Let's look at what happens when the Circle is freed from the Square. Remember that by definition, the Square is controlling. This is how the Square works. It comes up with strategies to produce predictable results.

When the Square leads, it dominates the Circle, as shown below.

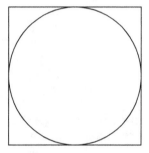

But what happens if the Circle exits the Square and becomes free? Let's look at the image below.

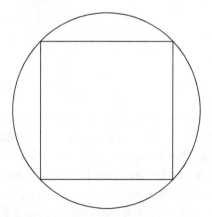

Will the Circle dominate the Square?

Actually, it won't. Why? **Once freed of the Square, the Circle will fully regain its creative, intuitive, agile, and holistic qualities.** It doesn't seek power or dominance. It's emergent. It seeks creativity and inclusivity. The Circle, just like nature, is creative and, as such, expansive. Even as it expands, it makes more space for the Square.

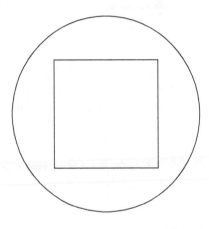

In turn, the Square, which by design seeks control, will expand in order to fulfill its purpose: to produce new knowledge and bring order. It keeps organizing the new space that it's given. This happens in every human organization, whether we're talking about civil societies, corporations, or families. The bigger the group, the more rules and processes it produces. Due to our Square bias, we have a hard time with anything that's not organized or unknown. Because we associate the nonrational with the irrational, we believe that what's not organized is disorganized and, therefore, not under control. As such, things that are not organized or easy to understand conjure fear in us. This is why we have a deep-seated tendency to seek control.

how it truly works

non-rational is *not* irrational

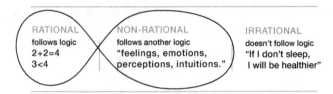

RATIONAL
follows logic
2+2=4
3<4

NON-RATIONAL
follows another logic
"feelings, emotions,
perceptions, intuitions."

IRRATIONAL
doesn't follow logic
"If I don't sleep,
I will be healthier"

Whereas in fact, if we relinquish control over the process there is the potential for a winning interaction between the Square and the Circle, in which both can expand and fulfill their respective purposes.

As a result the Circle is freed from the Square, which is best represented by the diagram below.

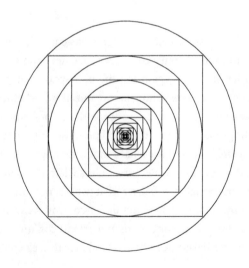

In this image, the Circle's qualities are freed to advance us further and help us gain additional perspective; discover new meanings; create what's next; and facilitate layered, deeper thinking for the most holistic decision-making process. The interaction between the Square and the Circle is endless by design and produces endless possibilities. It catalyzes solutions by following a natural instinctual process that is already in us.

SQUARE + CIRCLE = SQUIRCLE

SQUIRCLE
makes sense of what
doesn't make sense

With SQUIRCLE, nothing new needs to be learned. If anything, it's more about *unlearning* what we've learned. We all know better than what we were taught. The only requirement for us to improve under SQUIRCLE is a change of attitude. We need to let go of our long cultural habit of engaging life through the Square, of seeking control over the unknown. For this, we need to be able to tolerate uncertainty and vulnerability, as well as harness personal courage and patience. It's hard for most of us, but it's possible for *all* of us. This revolutionary mindset is called the **SQUIRCLE Attitude, a new way of being for a new way of doing**. In any culture or society, even in the hardest of situations, we always have a choice to evolve beyond or resist the old way of doing things. Take the extreme situation of Nelson Mandela, the South African leader and anti-apartheid activist who was imprisoned for twenty-seven years and endured physical and emotional abuse while he grieved for his loved ones. He couldn't escape his physical prison, but he chose to escape the mental prison he could have built around himself out of outrage, bitterness, and resentment. When talking about his enemies, he said: "I realized that they could take everything from me except my mind and my heart. They couldn't take those things. Those things I still had control over. And I decided not to give them away." And, he added: "To make peace with an enemy one must work with that enemy, and that enemy becomes one's partner."[1] If Nelson Mandela was able to change, evolve, and grow, the rest of us, who are living in much less extreme circumstances, can certainly do it. Mandela had a brilliant mind; however, his intellect alone would not have liberated him. He needed his heart too. Together, the Square and the Circle have the power to liberate us and advance us in new directions. A kind of alchemy occurs when they combine, but we need to open ourselves up to the Circle and give it more than equal footing in order to be transformed.

As we have seen, approaching a situation through the Square will compromise what the Circle can offer, whereas entering the same situation through the Circle will enable the Square to contribute all it can. There is an innate order within SQUIRCLE: **The Circle comes first**. But it doesn't come first in an imposing, exclusive, or willful way. It's simply about an inner shift, a change of intention, an openness that is required in order for the creative force of the Circle to immediately emerge and be felt. Thanks to its inclusiveness, the Circle embraces the oneness of life that naturally balances out any form of hierarchy. When we choose to embrace the Circle, we really don't give up much besides our illusion of control over life, but we gain so much.

SQUIRCLE is a concept that is simple to understand, a tool designed to help us move away from a binary lens and fully adopt a holistic one. No model or categorization will ever be able to explain nature entirely because nature is not static and is constantly evolving. The ultimate goal of SQUIRCLE is to help us develop and thrive in a holistic culture to the point that we don't need SQUIRCLE glasses anymore. After a while, we will have embraced our innate Circle nature and will be able to look at and function in the world in a balanced way.

To achieve that shift away from the undue dominance of the Square, the first step is to let go of the idea of control, not as an act of faith but as a logical deduction. Even though it is hard to admit it, we know that anything can happen at any time, whether it's an earthquake, an illness, or a traffic accident. We must first accept this intellectually and then accustom ourselves to it emotionally. It might seem daunting, but there are practical ways to achieve this. Deep breathing reconnects us with the present moment, so that we can find silence and stillness. Meditation will gently calm your mind, even if you only meditate for five or ten minutes a day. Observing nature—be it a forest, an ocean, or a single flower—will help you realize that you are part of its design and not separate from it. It will give you a sense of belonging to a world that is bigger than your immediate circumstances, which usually brings inner calm. Engage in these day-to-day activities with an explorer's mindset, and stay open to discoveries and surprises. In chapters 8, 9, and 10, you will find more practical ways to bring a SQUIRCLE attitude to your life. The ultimate goal is to realize that we don't need control in order to flourish and to bring this new awareness to everything we do.

QUESTIONS

- Think of a recent decision you made, like buying a car or renting an apartment. What Square factors went into your decision? What Circle factors did? Would you have made a different decision if you had considered only Square or only Circle factors?
- Sit with someone who is different from you in some way and share a few things about each of you. What do you have in common? How do your differences affect your relationship? Are these Square or Circle differences? We will talk more about how the Square and the Circle influence our personal interactions in chapter 9.

Square and Circle Together

S QUIRCLE represents the best of both the Square and the Circle; when combined the whole is greater than the sum of the parts, meaning that SQUIRCLE has unique power and advantages that neither the Square nor the Circle possess on their own. From the synergy between a nondominant Square and a liberated Circle are born SQUIRCLE solutions. To illustrate this concept, let's take a look at nine examples of SQUIRCLE Thinking at work in the modern world, in various fields. Each example shows that when Square perspectives are taken to the extreme, they can block out Circle realities and contributions; as a result, the impact of a dominant Square becomes negative. However, the same examples show the possibility of rebalancing their interaction for better outcomes:

- Energy;
- Fashion;
- Agriculture;
- Plastic;
- Performance Management;
- Productivity;
- Finance;
- Business;
- Organizational Design.

Some readers may find the first three examples enough to make the point, and skip to chapter 6. Idea-lovers, read on to further discover the benefits of SQUIRCLE Thinking through six additional examples.

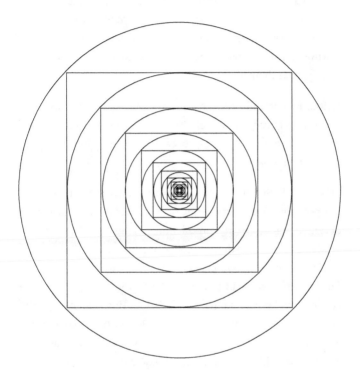

SQUIRCLE

When Square and Circle work in synergy for better outcomes

ENERGY

SQUARE: Humans invented electrical plants in the 1880s to produce electricity from coal. Today we know that these plants are massively contributing to both air pollution and global warming. This is why countries like Germany have decided to simply close them all by 2038[1].

CIRCLE: For millennia, sailboats have used wind energy, a natural resource, to propel themselves. Today wind is used mostly for pleasure boating because it is too slow to power commercial boats.

SQUIRCLE: Building on the idea of ocean winds as a renewable, nonpolluting source of energy, offshore wind farms have been designed for electricity production. Higher wind speeds are available offshore, so these wind farms generate a higher amount of electricity per capita installed than they would on land.[2] In Europe, offshore wind power has been price-competitive with conventional power sources since 2017.[3] This is an example of renewable energy—that is, energy collected from sources that are naturally replenished on a human timescale, such as solar, wind, hydro, tidal, geothermal and biomass.

Out of the Square are
born logical solutions like:

Within the Circle are born
natural solutions like:

Electrical
Plant

Ocean
Winds

Offshore
Wind Farms

FASHION

SQUARE: Cheaper and more convenient, synthetic fabrics like polyester were invented to make fashion accessible and practical. And it worked. The industry thrives on providing consumers with the latest trends at a rapid rate of turnover. This means, however, that each year we purchase approximately eighty items of clothing, a volume which inevitably puts strain on the planet in terms of resources and pollution.[4] Nearly three-fifths of all clothing ends up in incinerators or landfills within a year of being produced.[5]

CIRCLE: Around for more than seven thousand years, cotton is today the world's most commonly used natural fiber. While cotton is a natural fiber that can biodegrade at the end of its life, it is more expensive than polyester and also one of the most environmentally demanding crops. Cotton is "very water intensive to cultivate and process,"[6] taking between ten and twenty thousand gallons of water to make just a single pair of jeans and up to three thousand to make a T-shirt.

SQUIRCLE: Circulose is a new, scalable material made from recycled cotton clothes. It is a circular product, which means that it was intentionally designed to be restorative, using resources in multiple-use bio- or techno-cycles that still produce a high-quality product. Circulose preserves natural resources because it is a fabric created from waste. It is also vegan-friendly, nontoxic, durable, and biodegradable. With competitive pricing, it will help the fashion industry consume less high-impact cotton and synthetic fibers.[7] Combining natural fabric (Circle) with an efficient production process (Square), Circulose is a great SQUIRCLE solution.

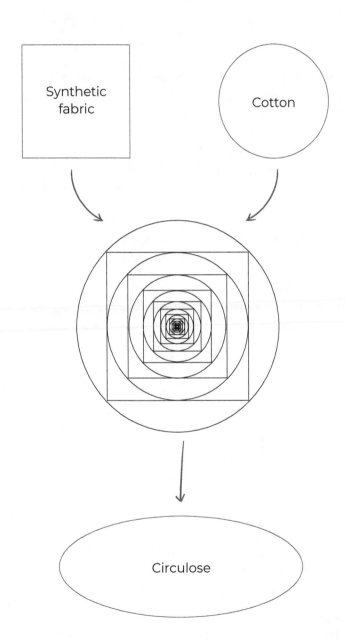

AGRICULTURE

SQUARE: To increase year-round food production for the world's population at affordable prices, we developed large-scale, intensive means of raising crops and animals, which often involve chemical fertilizers for crops or the routine use of antibiotics in livestock. While this system yields impressive amounts of food, it contributes to climate change, pollutes air and water, and depletes soil fertility. It also accounts for 80 percent of global deforestation[8].

CIRCLE: For millennia, humans hunted, fished, and picked foods found in nature to feed themselves.

SQUIRCLE: To offset the negatives of industrial agriculture, while still meeting necessary production levels[9], green agriculture was developed in the fifties and sixties. It incorporates ecological, organic, and conservation agriculture, as well as fair trade.

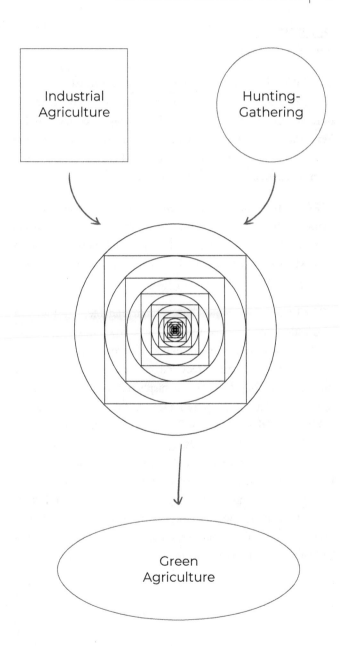

PLASTIC

SQUARE: The first synthetic plastic was invented in 1907 in New York State. Its advantages are many: it's water resistant, durable, strong, and economical. This is why it became popular. Yet today it pollutes the environment, threatens wildlife and oceans, and is very slow to degrade. Plastic can also emit harmful chemicals, especially if burned.

CIRCLE: In addition to excellent resistance to wear and tear, natural rubber derived from the latex sap of tropical trees offers good flexibility and is easy to fabricate, but it does not perform well when exposed to chemicals and petroleum derivatives, including petrochemicals.

SQUIRCLE: We now have biodegradable plastics, or bioplastics, that take less time to break down when discarded; are made from renewable resources like corn oil, orange peel, starch, and plants; can be recycled; and are less toxic than their predecessors. They don't contain bisphenol A (BPA), a hormone disrupter that is often found in traditional plastics. A 2017 study published by the Institute of Physics showed that if traditional plastics were produced using renewable energy sources, greenhouse gas emissions could be reduced by 50 to 75 percent; however, bioplastics produced with renewable energy showed even greater promise in this regard.[10] Nevertheless, new clean technology makes possible the industrial-scale production of commercial bio-based plastics, indicates new research from the University of Nebraska-Lincoln and Jiangnan University[11].

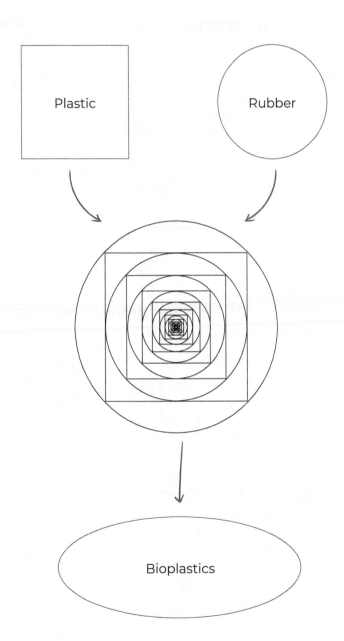

PERFORMANCE MANAGEMENT

SQUARE: Key Performance Indicators (KPI) were invented to improve employee performance. Since KPIs only show progress levels, it can be difficult to track the quality of the employee's work, which in turn may affect employee motivation as well as customer loyalty. These evaluations should be approached with caution because business itself is human by nature and humans are naturally not linear but complex. Business also requires creativity and agility, which flourish best with a certain degree of freedom and autonomy and are much harder to "quantify" or measure.

CIRCLE: Parents care for their children's minds, bodies, and souls, even as they allow them the freedom to experiment, succeed, and sometimes fail. They do not need KPIs to track and evaluate their children, or inspire them to do their best.

SQUIRCLE: Born out of the need to create more agile, innovative, and effective organizations, self-management in business means that once employees receive direction, they complete their own tasks, run their own projects, and try to solve their own problems. The manager's contact with reports generally consists of meetings for project updates, issue resolution, and resource requests. Experts say that for this method to be effective, employees need to understand why they're doing what they're asked to do, as well as the deeper meaning (or purpose) behind the assignment, rather than just blindly following directions.

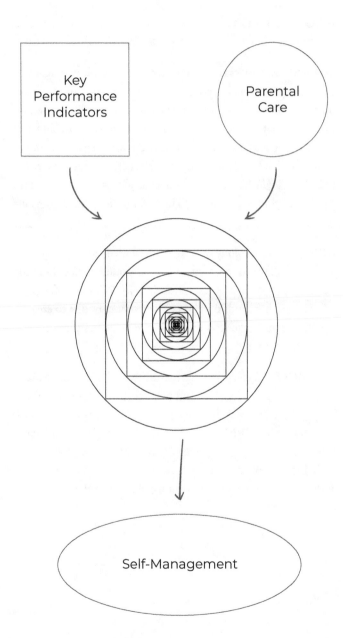

PRODUCTIVITY

SQUARE: Taylorism is one of the earliest scientific management theories, put forth by Frederick Taylor in the late 1890s to increase efficiency and productivity in factories. It focused on the belief that making people work as hard as they could was not as efficient as optimizing the way the work was done. Taylor proposed that by simplifying jobs, productivity would increase. Critics of Taylorism assert that it aims at turning workers into robots, machines, or objects, which is problematic for obvious reasons.

CIRCLE: Give a colony of garden ants a week and a pile of dirt, and they will transform it into an underground edifice about the height of a skyscraper in an ant-scaled city. Without a blueprint or a leader, thousands of insects move specks of dirt to create a complex, spongelike structure with parallel levels connected by a network of tunnels.

SQUIRCLE: Modern management theories see organizations as living organisms and complex adaptive systems. These "living organizations" have a dynamic relationship with their environment, and strive to grow and develop while at the same time enhancing each member of their ecosystem, unleashing each individual's and group's natural capacity for innovation and success, thereby outperforming planned and standardized productivity.

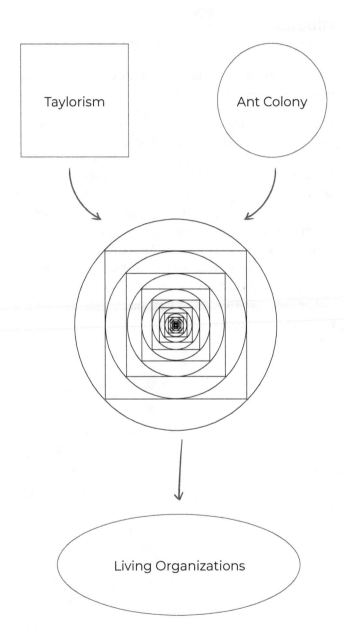

FINANCE

SQUARE: Banks lend to people who show the most financial solvency in order to minimize their risk.

CIRCLE: Charitable initiatives provide to those in need with the assumption that they cannot help themselves.

SQUIRCLE: Grameen America is a nonprofit organization that helps women on the fringe of poverty turn their lives around and become financially self-reliant through entrepreneurship by offering microloans, a community, and an emergent sense of purpose. In ten years, Grameen America has helped 129,000 women create 135,000 jobs and has distributed $1.42 billion in microloans. The reliability rate of these borrowers with very limited means is 99 percent, which is much higher than what is typically seen in regular banking[14].

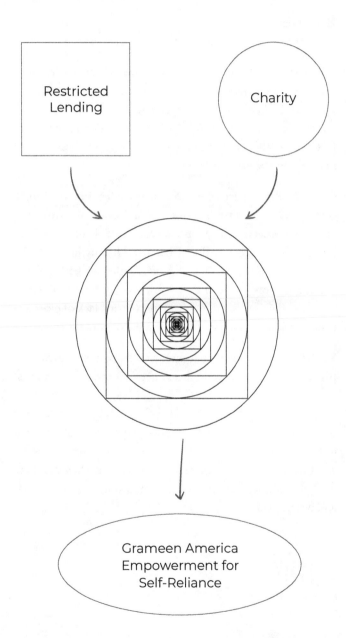

BUSINESS

SQUARE: The twentieth-century model of consumer goods and services companies relied on hiring employees and selling products in brick-and-mortar stores. This model was both capital- and labor-intensive, making it harder to start and maintain a business due to the costs of high seed capital and monthly overhead.

CIRCLE: Bartering is the oldest form of commerce. People would trade what they had to offer—a good or service—with others for whatever they wished to acquire. It didn't require a store or starting capital, but bartering has its limits. To be successful, it must result in the satisfaction of both parties, and this can only happen if the items bartered are realistically valued as the same by those involved. Often a lack of objective benchmarks makes it hard to agree on the value of the exchange.

SQUIRCLE: The "sharing economy" is an economic system in which assets or services are shared between private individuals, either for free or for a fee, typically by means of the internet. It requires no investment and no operating structure, yet transactions are easy, and the model is very profitable. Thanks to the sharing economy, you can easily rent out your car, your apartment, your bike, even your Wi-Fi network when you don't need it, and monetize assets that would otherwise depreciate and be an expense.

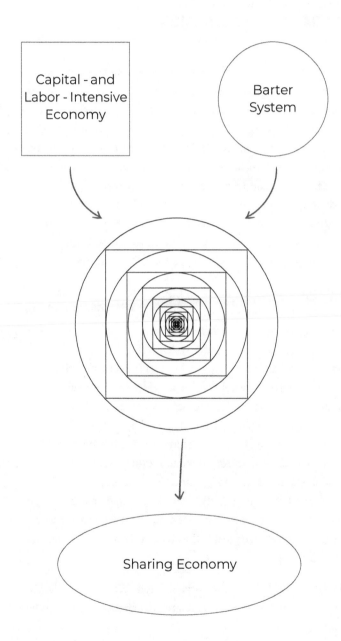

ORGANIZATIONAL DESIGN

SQUARE: Human organizations have long been viewed as hierarchical, orderly systems, the traditional way to organize large corporations or associations. This system relies on a vertical structure, often visualized as a pyramid, in which every person is subordinate to another individual or entity—except the one at the top. That person appears at the top of the structure, with direct reports and teams underneath in descending order. For example, the organization of the Catholic Church consists of the pope, then the cardinals, then the archbishops, and so on. Members of hierarchical organizational structures communicate chiefly with their immediate superior and subordinates.

CIRCLE: Nature is understood by science as both chaos and order, or order and disorder, at once. Fish schools, bird flocks, and animal herds are three examples of order that emerge from nature's self-organizing systems. Turbulent winds are an example of disorder that randomly produces beautiful sand dunes. Similarly, icy cold weather arrives suddenly and freezes atmospheric water vapor into light, white snowflakes, resulting in perhaps two inches of snowfall, perhaps ten. And yet, over time, we have realized that there is a predictability in these occurrences. *Chaos theory* is about finding underlying patterns in systems that appear to be disordered. Pulitzer Prize–winning author and cognitive scientist Douglas Hofstadter said, "It turns out that an eerie type of chaos can lurk just behind a facade of order—and yet, deep inside the chaos lurks an even eerier type of order."[12]

SQUIRCLE: A "chaordic" organization refers to a system of organization that blends characteristics of both chaos and order,

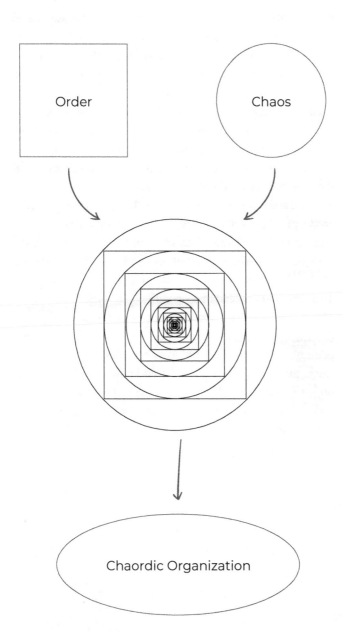

and is neither centralized nor anarchical. The term was coined by Dee Hock, the founder and former CEO at Visa Credit Cards. It was designed to simultaneously allow cooperation and competition among the member banks of the Visa-issuing network. This was necessary for the scale and universality needed to make credit cards usable in any geographic location and to provide a low cost for the processing of each transaction. The organization he created was indeed different. For example, instead of trying to enforce cooperation by restricting what the members could do, the Visa bylaws encouraged them to compete and innovate as much as possible. "Members are free to create, price, market, and service their own products under the Visa name," he explained in an article in *Fast Company*.[13] "At the same time, in a narrow band of activity essential to the success of the whole, they engage in the most intense cooperation." This harmonious blend of cooperation and competition is what allowed the system to expand worldwide in the face of different currencies, languages, legal codes, customs, cultures, and political philosophies. World Weather Watch and Alcoholics Anonymous are two other well-known and successful organizations that follow a comparable chaordic view. These organizations represent the coexistence of man-regulated order (Square) and natural chaos (Circle).

In the next chapter, through a direct personal experience, the SQUIRCLE Game, you will begin to discover what SQUIRCLE can bring to you in terms of interpersonal communication and collaboration, and how it can bolster your capacity to solve complex problems and make complex decisions to achieve your goals.

QUESTIONS

- Have you ever designed a new solution at home or at work that was more in balance with a Circle or SQUIRCLE approach?
- Can you identify other SQUIRCLE solutions that already exist in the "sharing economy," like Airbnb or Lyft, for instance?

The SQUIRCLE
Game

> You've achieved success in your field when
> you don't know whether what you're doing is
> work or play.
>
> —WARREN BEATTY

> Play is our brain's favorite way of learning.
>
> —DIANE ACKERMAN

W hen I do workshops for global companies, I often start without giving any introduction or explanation of what is going to happen over the course of the day. Instead, I invite everyone to play a game. The goal of the game is for workshop participants to take part in a group creative process designed to disrupt the status quo. To truly open ourselves up to creativity, we all require a certain level of physical relaxation to be present in our bodies, so I offer a playful activity that changes the space in the room and in the participants' minds in a relaxing and noncompetitive way. The game begins with the participants sitting in a circle in the center of a large room. Any tables have been removed or pushed to the four corners. First, I ask them to close their eyes and sit comfortably in their chairs. "Uncross your arms and your legs. Take a big breath and exhale slowly. Relax your abdomen. Relax your lower back, your middle back, your upper back. Relax your shoulders and neck. Relax your jaw muscles.

"Now please pay attention to your breathing. Notice a big muscle going up and down in your abdomen. This is your diaphragm. It goes up, putting pressure on your lungs, which then contract and push air out. This is Exhale. It goes down and makes space for your lungs to expand and pull in air. This is Inhale. Observe the movements of your diaphragm, going up and down. Be present to it. Savor the moment. This moment happens once. It will never happen again. Relax in it. Enjoy it."

After a few minutes, I ask them to open their eyes and connect visually with the space around them. The atmosphere in the room is already more relaxed. I then ask them what was truly extraordinary in this short experience. Usually someone will say, "I felt more relaxed than usual," another that she "felt present in a deeper way" than she's used to, and another that he was able to "slow down" the flow of thoughts in his head. I ask the same question again: "What was truly *extraordinary* in this short experience?" and more responses come. Eventually I share with them my own thoughts: "What's truly extraordinary is that this highly complex process of breathing involves millions, if not billions, of cells in your body. It happens from our first breath as a newborn until the last breath of our existence and never lets us down. It is absolutely essential to our survival, yet it happens without us thinking about it or trying to make it happen. This is not only totally remarkable, it is also proof that our bodies have an *extraordinary* instinctual, natural ability to manage very complex processes and challenges. Let's see how we can tap into this ability to solve complex problems as a group."

In the second part of the game, I tell the participants to take off their shoes, stand up, and push their chairs against the wall. "Walk around the room randomly," I tell them. "Feel free to jump, move your arms, walk as fast or slow as you wish. Make sounds, speak up and say whatever your body feels like. Keep moving! Now stop. Stay where you are, look straight ahead, don't turn your head to me, and close your eyes."

The participants are now standing, eyes closed. They have no shoes on. They have little or no clue about where the others are standing or what they will be asked to do next. "Now," I continue, "I will ask you to be silent."

When they are quiet, I give them instructions for the third part, which is the game itself. "You are going to recite, as a group, the English alphabet from A to Z. One person will speak a letter, then another person will say the next one, and so on. You can say as many letters as you want during the game, but only one letter at a time. Order of participation is totally random, and you have to strictly follow the alphabetical order, without any repeats. You can also participate by remaining fully silent, as long as the group completes the alphabet. But if two people speak at the same time, or the group doesn't follow the alphabetical order, you will need to start all over again. That is the hard part!"

Usually people laugh after hearing this. Then the room grows quiet again. Silence builds. Finally, a voice is heard: "A." The room is quiet. Then another participant says, "B." Silence returns. We hear another voice say "C." Some participants always try to outsmart the exercise by speaking right after another person. Trained to be analytical and results-oriented by their professions, and competitive by our culture, they try to get around the confusion they feel, standing there in their stocking feet with their eyes closed, with no way to predict who is going to speak next or to be sure of when it will be a good time to attempt a letter. The ambiguity can be difficult to bear; for some, even just keeping their eyes closed for a long stretch of time is uncomfortable. Often they feel a nervous need to be more productive because simply standing still doesn't feel efficient enough. Eventually, another participant dares a *D* and then, from somewhere in the group, another one rushes to say "E." Unfortunately, somebody else tries the same trick and a second *E* tumbles out at the same time. The group has to start all over again.

Usually after a few tries, the group begins to feel heavy with frustration and somewhat lost. Then and only then do I give them new instructions: "Try to breathe deeply and calm down. Feel what's going on in the room around you, even if you cannot see anything, and allow yourselves to play, like a five-year-old. Give up the goal of reaching *Z*. Stay in the moment, connected to your breathing. Simply enjoy the process."

The game starts again. As always, a participant tries once more to beat the process and make the group reach *Z* faster. Almost systematically, it does not work. A few letters later two participants speak at the same time. Back to *A*.

There is no way to succeed at the game by forcing it. Everyone depends on each other, so everybody needs to give up individual control and allow a natural rhythm to emerge from the group. When participants start to relax, to enjoy the challenge without any fear of negative consequences, they begin to make progress without trying. Letting go of the outcome and relinquishing control feel less daunting. They become immersed in the process and the natural flow among them. It takes self-confidence, trust, deep inner listening, and a different kind of concentration—a state in which they are both focused and relaxed at the same time. With proper guidance, most groups manage to get to *Z*—with great celebration!

When time allows, I ask the participants to do the exercise a second time with more distance between them, so that they are even more isolated from one another. Later in the workshop, when the group has made substantial progress, I sometimes ask them to block their ears with their fingers or earplugs. This way they can't anticipate when someone is going to speak by listening to the sound of their breathing. At this point, participants have to rely solely on their intuition. The exercise seems impossible, yet when practiced regularly, a different type of listening develops and something extraordinary takes place. When the group dynamic is good, there is no particular order to the sequence of voices, and yet a uniting factor sustains and facilitates an "orderly" process. Everyone becomes calm. Quietly, resolutely, the letters of the alphabet are enunciated one by one, from *A* to *Z*. When a group makes it to the end, all faces are happy.

The synchronicity of a real team

To be able to work together as a group without any one particular leader, in the heat of the action and under the pressure of trying to reach a definite goal, is when you know you have a real team. You are working together with the same type of rapport that actors cultivate to create an evening of theatrical greatness or that a basketball team uses to deliver a masterful game. The phenomenon that takes place can be likened to the neural synchronization—that is, the correlated appearance of neuronal activity, from a single cell to the whole brain—that occurs between two or more people and has been demonstrated in neuroscience experiments. Something as simple as an everyday conversation causes people's brains to begin to work simultaneously. This was the conclusion of a study carried out by the Basque Centre on Cognition, Brain, and Language (BCBL), and published in 2017 in the magazine *Scientific Reports.*[1] Researchers simultaneously analyzed the neuronal activity of two strangers who held a dialogue for the first time. By recording the subjects' cerebral electrical activity, they confirmed that the neuronal activity of two people involved in an act of communication "synchronizes" in order to allow for a connection between them. "[Dialogue] involves interbrain communion that goes beyond language itself and may constitute a key factor in interpersonal relations and the understanding of language," explained one of the lead researchers of the study.

What this means for work and for life in general is that cooperative communication between people is made possible by a natural, subconscious brain function as much as by our own conscious effort. In our culture, we focus on what's being said outwardly (Square), but there's much more going on beneath the surface (Circle). The good news is that we can tap into these intangible yet real dynamics to have more effective meetings or discussions, to deepen our thinking, solve complex challenges, and unveil new possibilities (SQUIRCLE). To do so, we must not only give up control over the process but also realize that we don't *need* to control it to achieve a positive outcome.

Meditation can help us shift away from listening to the meaning of spoken words in order to hear the subtle cues beneath them. George Burr Leonard, the author of numerous books on developing human potential, writes in his seminal book *The Silent Pulse*, "Meditation helps us become more sensitive to our vibrations and inner rhythms . . . [and] find ourselves in a great state of harmony with our environment and people around us." Likewise, in her book *My Stroke of Insight*, neuroanatomist Jill Bolte Taylor describes how a severe stroke led her to discover that the more time she spent running on the deep circuitry of her brain's right hemisphere, which is responsible for the processing of visual and audio stimuli, as well as artistic ability, the more likely she was to experience oneness with those around her. Both authors assert that we can access this potential for deeper listening and connecting with others through focus and practice. A medical study published by the National Institutes of Health evidenced the benefits of meditation resulting in more focus and thickened brains in practitioners[2]. Comparable results for attendees to an eight-week meditation course were relayed in an article in the Harvard Gazette Health and Medicine section, titled *When Science meets mindfulness.*[3]

The SQUIRCLE Game and real life

The SQUIRCLE Game perfectly mirrors situations that arise in everyday life: something needs to get done (getting to Z), but we have no idea as to how to go about it. Sometimes we're unable to ask for advice from a team member when we need to make this important decision or achieve this goal, like every player in the game; sometimes we fully depend on others to produce results, like participants in the game. We may not necessarily share the same values or opinions about how to deal with the situation but forcing our way on the group is a short-lived strategy that will not strengthen our ability to collaborate on or achieve our goal.

During the SQUIRCLE Game, we can clearly see two approaches at play. One consists of exerting efforts and attempting different strategies to win—the Square approach. The other involves relinquishing control, going with the flow, and opening up to sensations and emotions to navigate the unknown—the Circle approach. In a complex situation, the first one (Square) does not work; the other (Circle) does. I have seen groups force their way through to Z and succeed. However, these groups were not able to repeat their feat, and no sense of team cohesiveness had been gained. Ironically, it was more a stroke of luck than anything else, and you cannot succeed in business or in life on luck alone. This game helps players redefine their approach to success and understand how to use the SQUIRCLE attitude when trying to navigate a situation or environment that they cannot control.

The only group of people I have ever worked with that was able to complete the SQUIRCLE Game in one go was in Tokyo. All the participants were Japanese. Over the years, I have facilitated this game on five continents with people of approximately sixty different nationalities, and I had never seen this happen before, so I was eager to ask the participants what the game had felt like and to what they attributed their win. Two factors emerged: social discretion is paramount in Japanese society, and is best demonstrated through silence. Japanese people value silence highly as a fundamental form of nonverbal communication and associate it with truthfulness. For them, even more than language, silence conveys information, emotions, and rich and ambiguous subtleties, which in turn forces attentive listening. In my many years of doing business in Japan, I had meetings where the CEO would listen quietly while his team members talked about the details of a transaction or even things totally unrelated to business.

In the West, it's usually the opposite: the lower you are in the hierarchy, the less you are expected to talk in meetings, and for the sake of efficiency, small talk is rather limited.

The idea that an underlying force in you, let alone one among a group, can emerge to achieve more than you could through intense, willful, consciously directed effort remains, in our

Western culture, a very foreign concept for individuals and organizations. Often, I hear people say that they initially felt self-conscious during the game or concerned that they were not participating or trying hard enough. They forced themselves to jump in, but doing so only caused the group to fail. It's hard to accept the idea that we have to give up command and control to find the best solution to a complex challenge, yet within a day or two of the workshop, participants realize results for their goals and recognize that it works, even if they can't fully comprehend how it happens. Remember that nature manifests everything in the same way. Trees produce oxygen when they use energy from sunlight, but they don't try or intend to do so, they just do. Likewise, clients have reported that choosing a leadership of influence over one of control helps them to communicate better and resolve difficult problems more easily. Still, the only way for you to truly know if it works is to try it for yourself.

Here are four radical takeaways from the SQUIRCLE Game that can help you unlock your innate potential, both at work and in your personal life.

Lesson #1: To access your natural ability to solve a complex problem, you need to give up control of the mind.

The SQUIRCLE Game is complex! Not because what you're being asked to do—recite the alphabet—is so difficult, but because you're being asked to do a simple thing while giving up control. In a situation like this, emotions like frustration, discomfort, and discouragement can rear their heads. Our bodies get tense, and we become even more uncomfortable. Our inclination is to find a strategy *out* of the situation—"I'll say a letter RIGHT after someone else," or, "No one has said anything for a while. I'll go NOW"—rather than exploring a new path *through* the difficulty. As a culture, we are so used to command and control that participants in the game never doubt that a proactive plan of action will deliver the expected result: reaching Z. But it almost never happens, because when asked to repeat their feat, they have nothing to build on. I have never seen a group succeed twice in a row by using a mental strategy, but what I have seen work every time is when participants *relinquish mental control over the process.* It is only when participants give up on strategy and choose to stay in the moment and open themselves completely that they complete the task. So how is this accomplished?

The simplest way to be in the moment is to pay attention and focus on your breathing. When we are present to our breath, the mental chatter quiets down. You are not thinking about the past or the future or even the task at hand; paying attention to your breathing pulls you directly into the present moment and makes space for other natural abilities to emerge. Every group that I have worked with reports that when they concentrate on breathing, they move from a competitive mindset that seeks control over the situation to a more open, collaborative approach. A form of subtle, nonverbal communication begins to take place among the members that guides them in a tangible and measurable way toward solving the alphabet game.

> **Take-away #1: To confront complexity, keep your mind open and be flexible (CIRCLE), but use discipline (SQUARE) to engage your breath and stay present to the moment.**

Lesson #2: You can best communicate with others when you focus on yourself first.

What I hear and observe in every SQUIRCLE Game is that to access this level of subtle communication between players, a person must first connect with herself. This seems like a paradox and it is; in fact, we are usually taught to focus on others in order to connect. But if you don't listen carefully to yourself, it's going to be hard to pay attention to anyone else with equal care. This is similar to the instructions you receive on an airplane in the case of an emergency: you are told to first place an oxygen mask over your mouth before helping your children or anyone else.

When you listen to yourself you become naturally receptive to low signals in yourself *and* in others. Sports teams and actors do this all the time; through practice and repetition, they develop a deeper sensitivity to the other members of their team or cast, as well as a capacity to anticipate what's next without having to think about it. The SQUIRCLE Game teaches us to do exactly that. I have seen clients develop such an acute sensitivity to the process that they can actually predict what will happen next. One participant who had been practicing the SQUIRCLE Game with his team on a weekly basis over a few months told me that when the group reached *Y*, he could feel who would speak the final letter *Z*. He explained that, for him, it was a form of inner knowing that felt quite different from analytical thinking, and he was surprised

Paradox is a word derived from ancient Greek that literally means "what goes against" (para-) "commonly believed opinions" (doxa). But a paradox is not necessarily illogical; it is simply a counterintuitive proposition or statement that goes against what we typically believe.

to discover this ability within himself. Like him, we all have capacities beyond those that we typically allow ourselves to tap into in everyday life.

There is only one way to develop and retain this level of receptiveness: deliberate practice. For almost a year, I worked with a multinational team in Asia Pacific (APAC). They had different mother tongues and came from several places around the globe, yet they had a genuine desire to become a unified team with the indirect goal of improving performance. They regularly practiced and played the SQUIRCLE Game with focused attention, and when they couldn't meet physically, they would still do it over the phone, with each participant in their own country and time zone. As they got better at the game, they shared with me that they also saw enormous progress in their individual leadership styles, interpersonal relationships, team management, productivity, and business performance. The listening and receptivity they cultivated carried over naturally into their work and communications with other collaborators. They were able to impart some of this to their own leadership teams in their respective countries, creating a positive ripple effect. They reported better team performance and a boost in their creativity as well as their business results. At the end of the year that we worked together, they were asked by the global CEO to deliver 10 percent growth. The APAC president felt it was a tall order, but in the end, twelve months later, they delivered 20 percent growth compared to 8 percent industry market growth in APAC that year.

> **Take-away #2: You have the capacity for unspoken communication. Start by sharpening your sensitivity to yourself (CIRCLE) and then commit to practicing the SQUIRCLE Game regularly (SQUARE) with your family, friends, or colleagues to develop your sensitivity to others.**

Lesson #3: To get to this level of complex problem-solving, you need to suspend judgement.

This is the hard part. After participants attempt the SQUIRCLE Game for the first time, they often share their feelings of frustration, self-doubt, fear, or guilt about messing up the group process or not getting to the end quickly enough. They are often so preoccupied or unnerved that they lose patience or focus solely on winning what they imagine to be a competition. Once the dean of a renowned graduate school told me how surprised he was to see his fellow participants still competing to get to Z when they had been explicitly asked to give up the ambition of success and to simply play, aimlessly, with no intention other than having a good time, like five-year-olds at recess. He was amazed by their resistance to experiment with something new, to simply play and be.

It is hard to remain comfortable in the unknown with no plan of action. It is hard not only emotionally but also intellectually. In our society, it is considered a sign of weakness or foolishness to not have a plan to reach a measurable objective. Players often feel personally responsible for the success of the group, which leads to self-judgment, which then turns into controlling thoughts and behaviors, but if you cannot let go of the strategic mind, there's no way you can complete the SQUIRCLE Game. **And to let go of strategy, you have to let go of judgment.** In other words, you must adopt a beginner's mind. To be able to do this, you have to accept your negative emotions, such as frustration or anxiety. Let them come to the surface freely. Observe them for what they are. Because we feel the need to maintain control over our bodies, we usually try to manipulate our feelings with our mind—through pep talks, stories, recollections of how we effectively tackled similar situations previously, and so on—in order to get a handle on the situation.

The truth is that we don't control our body. Yes, we have to sleep when our body is tired and drink water when it is thirsty. We have to accept difficult emotions that arise, just as we have to accept rainstorms when we had planned an afternoon of hiking with our friends. What we can do, however, is **control our reaction to our body's sensations and emotions.** Don't judge them with thoughts like, "Confusion is bad," or, "I'm so frustrated, we'll never get this @#¶•! game done;" instead, simply recognize that you have them and let them go. This will put you in a better position to have a positive influence on your body and emotions, to reach an emotional balance called equanimity, and to be present in your body and the moment. This is when our natural abilities to solve complex issues surfaces within us. A creative aptitude that feels like a magic antidote to our binary, logical mind emerges and leads us down unexpected paths toward new solutions.

> **Take-away #3: Approach yourself as a forever evolving, open book (CIRCLE) and hone the discipline (SQUARE) to defer judgement.**

> **Lesson #4: You have all the answers in you. It's simply a matter of allowing yourself to experiment with the unknown.**

Remember that the SQUIRCLE Game is similar to most situations in life: you need to solve a complex problem and deliver a tangible solution within a certain amount of time; you have to interact with other people and negotiate their often-unpredictable actions and reactions; and you have to adapt to circumstances beyond your control that can change at any time. You have to accept the situation for what it is and feel your way through the process. You have to not only let go of your fear of failing, but also *commit to courageously experimenting.*

In her book *The Gardener and the Carpenter*, Alison Gopnik offers an organic approach to raising children. She attempts to persuade parents and educators to stop trying to mold children into adults with some desirable mix of characteristics the way a carpenter might build a cabinet from a set of plans. Instead, we adults should model ourselves on gardeners, who experiment with nature and create a nurturing ecosystem for children to flourish, but accept our limited ability to control or even predict the outcome. Rather than viewing parenting as an activity or skill to be mastered, adults should simply be parents and see it as an ongoing experimentation. As an article[4] in *The Atlantic* explained, "Her message is not: 'You are parenting wrong.' Her message is, 'If you do the things that come naturally to you [and allow yourself to experiment], that's the best formula for being a successful parent.'"

Experimenting is a necessary part of being alive. The human brain is plastic and has the potential to evolve based on the physical and mental activities that it is repeatedly involved in.[5] The SQUIRCLE Game is a tool that can **intentionally change our minds for the better, allowing our brains to function in a new and highly adaptive, innovative way.**

As with any science experiment, **you must commit to challenging your assumptions and focusing on the process, not the outcome.** But a true experimenter's mindset is not about being optimistic or pessimistic because this would mean that you are judging particular paths. Your responsibility is to be neither overwhelmed by the unknown nor satisfied with the status quo. You must harness courage, an open mind, and a willingness to pioneer uncharted territories. Faith in yourself and the abilities that are wired naturally inside you is the foundation.

> **Take-away #4: Experimentation is the best path through the unknown. Trust your instinct to guide you, and trust your natural capacity for adaptation.**

FOR SQUIRCLE SUCCESS

- Give up control
- Sharpen your sensitivity to yourself
- Suspend judgment
- Commit to experimentation

QUESTIONS

- Can you think of instances in which you (and others) have given up personal control and let the group work things out? How did that turn out? How did you feel?
- Have you ever taken an improv class? Were you able to stay in the moment? How did you feel?
- Could you and a friend practice suspending judgment fully for five minutes while discussing a movie about which you have different opinions? This can be more challenging than it seems ... practice!
- How often do you experiment at work or at home with friends or your kids? Changing your routines, for instance, to see how this change affects you and others? Do you like it?

What is your SQUIRCLE Preference?

Always remember that you're absolutely
unique. Just like everyone else.

— MARGARET MEAD

There is an ocean of creativity within
every human being.

— DAVID LYNCH

We all function with varying degrees of Square and Circle approaches to life. In this chapter, I have put together a simple test to help you reflect on your relative preferences for Square and Circle. The purpose of this test is not to assign you to a specific profile or category; it is merely meant to foster self-reflection and promote open discussion with others. If you understand your preferences and those of other people, you can use this knowledge to optimize outcomes in both your personal and professional lives.

Taking now a quick break from reading this book will deliver results for you. In only a few minutes you will have completed the short questionnaire and will receive a long report. It will include an in-depth analysis of all different types, insights about yourself and people around you, actionable tips to implement immediately, and the opportunity to join a community of other SQUIRCLE participants or invite others you know to this community of individuals committed to learning and evolving.

Your SQUIRCLE preference is not about:

- *Creativity vs. rigidness*
- *Productivity vs. dreaming*
- *Good vs. bad*

It is simply a conversation starter with yourself, your partner, your work teams, and/or your friends.

The SQUIRCLE Test and its results are based on years of administering assessments worldwide. Through my work with clients, I have identified seven profiles: three Square preferences (Strong, Clear, and Slight), three Circle preferences (Strong, Clear, and Slight), and one in which Square and Circle are preferred equally. Strong, Clear, and Slight are indications of how much you may lean toward Square or Circle at the time you answer the questionnaire. Your SQUIRCLE preference will vary according to your age and life experience, the job you occupy, the people you are surrounded by at home or at work, the type of business culture you operate in, and even the community in which you live.

It should take you only a few minutes to answer the questions, and there are no right or wrong answers. The SQUIRCLE Test is not a pass-or-fail type of exam. It is simply an assessment of your orientation to life. The more openly you respond, the deeper the insights you will receive. If you are unsure about how to answer a question, think of yourself when you're at your most natural and vulnerable, for instance, when you play, when you interact with people you trust, or when you were a child and filled with spontaneity and openhearted wonder about the world and the people in it.

Before you begin, here are the answers to a few frequently asked questions.

How will the SQUIRCLE Test help me?

The SQUIRCLE Test helps you assess whether you tend to be analytical and structured when approaching decisions, challenges, interpersonal communication, and collaborations, or if you tend to be flexible and adaptable and keep your options open as long as possible before making a move.

How should I use the SQUIRCLE Test results?

The SQUIRCLE Test results are meant to trigger self-reflection and insights into others, not to put anyone in a fixed category. SQUIRCLE should not be used as a tool to screen candidates for a job or decide who gets a promotion at work. It is not designed to ban two people from working together or from being in a romantic relationship. A person's suitability for a particular job or collaboration depends on the person's skill set, experience, personality, and self-awareness. SQUIRCLE aims to help you with the latter and give you a better understanding of others. It can, however, be used to assemble or balance teams for different tasks such as an innovative project or a cost-cutting initiative.

Are the SQUIRCLE results affected in any way by gender, generation, or country?

While we have used our model with large, diverse audiences around the world, we have not conducted comparative research involving genders, cultures, or generations. Empirically, we have noticed that people in Western countries and northern countries around the globe respond differently to the SQUIRCLE Game than those in Eastern and southern countries. People from the latter group usually show a greater ability to go with the flow, and therefore the SQUIRCLE Game feels more natural to them. However, what is being offered in terms of the SQUIRCLE Test and how it facilitates behavioral change and attitude is universal and accessible to all.

Can I take the SQUIRCLE Test more than once?

Our website currently allows one test per email address. If you have a second email you can take it again, which may be helpful if you find yourself in different circumstances such as a new job or a major lifestyle change.

Where can I find specific guidance for me, based on my SQUIRCLE profile?

In addition to the information provided in chapters 8, 9, and 10, SQUIRCLE Academy offers a number of resources, including e-courses, webinars, and coaching for your SQUIRCLE type. You'll find courses on different topics including SQUIRCLE TIME, SQUIRCLE PRODUCTIVITY, SQUIRCLE COLLABORATION, SQUIRCLE YOU, SQUIRCLE MASTER, and more at:

www.squircleacademy.com.

How can I get my boss to give our entire team the SQUIRCLE Test?

If you think your boss might be more of a Square profile, I would highlight the progress you could potentially make in terms of performance and productivity by putting together complementary teams of Square, Circle, and Even profiles. I would also give your boss the SQUIRCLE Guide, which explains how the approach has helped two hundred and fifty thousand Fortune 500 executives as well as business students at prestigious schools around the world.

If you think your boss might be more of a Circle profile, you can share the exercise in which you think of words associated with the Square and the Circle. Then you can share the story of Emma and the parrot. That should be enough to start a conversation about creativity and agility and about how SQUIRCLE can help unleash them in your organization.

I'm a Circle and am tired of having my ideas ignored because they're too "wacky" or "out there." Help!

You're not alone! This happens to many people with a strong Circle profile. Here's what I suggest: try to find a colleague with an Even profile and ask them to be a sounding board for your three best creative ideas. After you've explained what they are, ask them to repeat back to you what they heard and understood. This process is useful because you will get a chance to see how they process and react to your information. From there, you will be in a better position to present your ideas in a way that is optimally suited to the thought process of an Even type. If it is only recently that you have had this type of response to your ideas, you can also ask a Square profile. Either way, doing so will help you find a way to express your ideas in a manner that comes across as reasonable enough to be valued and tested. Good luck!

I'm a Square and desperately want to find more time to develop my creative side. How can I do this?

Here are a few things you can try: Change your routine in the morning. Explore new foods for breakfast or other meals. Search for a new route to travel to work or to your school. Change your podcast subscription or try new radio programs; different hosts and shows will bring new ideas and viewpoints to you. Making these changes might feel uncomfortable at first, but stick with it. Even these subtle shifts away from the familiar can bring new colors and perspectives to your life. You might find that you feel rejuvenated or energized.

If just thinking about this kind of change feels like too much to do on your own, pick a friend that you suspect has a Circle or Even profile and ask them what they do to spark and express their creativity. You can even ask a few friends until you've learned about at least three things that you'd like to try, either with them or on your own. Make yourself accountable in a way that will help. You can, for instance, keep a log of the changes you make and how you feel about them. If you enjoy them, you will undoubtedly gain confidence to push further into uncharted territories.

I'd like to put together a social group or a team at work based on our shared SQUIRCLE profiles. Any suggestions about what we might do for fun?

Yes! This type of group is a great way to facilitate useful peer-to-peer learning. Being part of a community provides support and offers a chance for you to share your similar perspectives and experiences with each other.

For Circles, play games like Cranium, Apples to Apples, or Balderdash. Take an improv class together or play improv games. Ask a local charity if they need creative problem solving and brainstorm ideas and help them develop these ideas into actionable solutions.

For Squares, host a Risk, Bridge, or Ticket to Ride tournament. Organize a football pool for your offices. Ask Circles if they need help to bring to completion a community project for the office that they have been working on for too long. Put together a 12-month master calendar with all the fun events for which you'd like to plan ahead something really special.

For Evens, join either a Circle or Square group and feel free to move between these groups. You'll find yourselves having great fun simply observing the differences from one group to the other. In addition, you will be very useful to either type.

Don't forget to invite people from your opposite profile every once in a while. You'll learn a lot about yourself, as will others.

I am a Square and would like to make sure Circle people in my life pay more attention to deadlines because I get anxious when people finish projects at the last minute.

It's a classic scenario. Like leaving for the airport with enough lead time or getting the group presentation to your boss ready one day before so that you have time to review it with a calm mind. It's challenging because often Circles function better under pressure or simply prefer to keep their options open to the last minute. So it is a matter of understanding their needs and finding ways for your mutual expectations to be respected for what they bring to the situation. Being ready ahead of time minimizes stress and mistakes. Leaving options open is good for creativity as the creative process yields its best insights whenever it does. These are real differences. The best way is to set time aside to discuss them with an open mind and revisit the issue on a regularly basis.

**Now, go online to www.squircleacademy.com and take the
test.** When you're finished, your personal preference will be
revealed. You'll receive an email with the same information that
you can download onto your device and revisit anytime you
want. You will also find a twenty-one-page SQUIRCLE Guide
that describes all seven profiles. Although by far most people
report that their test results match their style and approach
to life, I recommend, as you read the description of your
preference, that you highlight in green what seems correct and
highlight in red what feels less so. If you see much more green
than red, your profile is accurate, but if there is much more red
or a balance between red and green, then take a look at some of
the profiles close to yours, and as you read other profiles, repeat
the highlighting exercise. Your true preference will be wherever
you have the most green. If in doubt, you can ask the opinions
of people who are close to you and who have known you for a
while and seen you in a variety of situations. It may help you to
hear their feedback and to discuss their perception of you.

Once you're familiar with your own preference, ask others to
take the test, and then share and discuss your respective results.
We tend to learn the most about ourselves and each other when
we can have an open discussion about how and why we feel and
do what we do.

QUESTIONS

- Now that you've taken the test, did your preference match your perception of yourself? What does your best friend have to say about it?
- Try to guess your best friend's or your family members' SQUIRCLE profiles. On what did you base your guesses? Next, ask them to take the quiz and see if you were correct!

SQUIRCLE
& You

> Know thyself.
>
> — DELPHIC MAXIM

> The illiterate of the twenty-first century will not be those who cannot read and write, but those who cannot learn, unlearn, and relearn.
>
> — ALVIN TOFFLER

By now, you hopefully understand that even though we live in a world where the Square dominates the Circle, we all need to create a synergy between Square and Circle approaches in order to succeed. This synergy is achieved when the interaction between the Square and the Circle produces a combined effect that is greater and more powerful than their effects are separately. For this to happen, our collective responsibility is to make sure that Square qualities (e.g., rational, dependable, optimizing) support Circle qualities (creative, agile, flexible, and so on). As we have seen, the cost of emphasizing and reinforcing the Square mindset is very high in terms of adaptation, innovation, sustainability, gender equality, and our ability to make complex decisions that solve problems. However, we also saw in chapter 5 what SQUIRCLE synergy can deliver in terms of energy production, agriculture, office productivity, and many other areas of society that need fresh ideas and groundbreaking solutions.

It's essential that all of us, no matter what we scored on the SQUIRCLE Test, understand how the Circle, as a creative force, can enrich our lives and how the Square, as an extremely efficient tool, can provide structure and objectivity in a positive way. Equally important is to keep in mind that any tool is ultimately designed to enable progress and unleash possibilities, not to hold them back. Our use of science (Square) is meant to make life safer and easier for humans in nature (Circle), not *in spite of* nature. The following are quick and easy markers that you can use to determine whether you are achieving adequate synergy between the Circle and the Square. Over the years, I've seen these markers work well when used by executives operating in high-pressure, demanding environments; in any given situation, at any point in time, you can use these as a checklist to make sure that you are incorporating both. Here are three measures of a well-honed Circle approach.

1. How in touch you are with your emotions. Any time you try to push away an emotion, you compromise your entire emotional circuit. As discussed in chapter 4, research shows that our emotions open us up to the nuances and subtle perceptions that are key to complex decision-making. They are a link between our body and mind, between reason and instinct. In other words, by disconnecting yourself from even one single emotion, you risk disconnecting yourself from your instinct and its wealth of creativity and agility. Emotions are also closely linked to physical sensations; in my client seminars, we offer silly games at the beginning, like throwing a soft ball around, drawing your portrait with your hand, pen, and paper inside a paper bag, or faking karate movements (*katas*) to get people more physically engaged. When they are relaxed and having fun, they become more emotionally open. These activities are more than icebreakers. They actually serve as a launchpad for deeper communication and trust.

In chapter 6, we talked about how acknowledging your emotions allows you to reach equanimity, or emotional balance, which will in turn improve your ability to communicate and collaborate effectively with others. Being aware of how you're likely to respond to certain situations and knowing how to manage those feelings responsibly puts you in a better position to be less afraid and to be able to respond to whatever life throws at you. You will be less daunted by difficult decisions and more positive about potential outcomes, all of which contribute to better relationships with those around you. A scientific study published in the *International Journal of Organization Analysis* provides empirical evidence that the individual's capacity to understand and manage emotions is positively related to the individual's influence on team decisions.[1] Team-level emotional intelligence (Circle) improves team decision-making performance (Square) through increases in psychological safety. This in turn encourages trust, risk-taking, and experimentation. Trust is the foundation of any functional team, and risk-taking is necessary for experimentation, which, as we've seen, directly enables us to innovate and chart new paths into the unknown.

SIX STEPS TO MINDFULLY DEAL WITH EMOTIONS

1. Turn toward your emotions with acceptance.

Become aware of the emotion and identify where you sense it in your body.

2. Identify and label the emotion.

To stay mindful, say to yourself, "This is anger" or "This is anxiety."

3. Accept your emotions.

Don't deny the emotion. Acknowledge and accept that it is there.

4. Realize the impermanence of your emotions.

Even if the emotion feels overwhelming, remember that it will pass.

5. Inquire and investigate.

Ask yourself, "What triggered me? Why do I feel this way?"

6. Let go of the need to control your emotions.

Be open to the outcome of your emotions and what unfolds.

Credit: The Gottman Institute

2. How much you play and, more importantly, how much you allow yourself to have a playful approach to serious situations. Play is a profound biological process,[2] an instinctive act that frees us from the grip of instinct at the same time. Imagine that your young child is sitting in the back seat of your car, crying for food. You are on a long trip, and it is midnight. You have one more hour to drive before you reach home. There is no food in the car, and stores are closed. What can you do to appease your child? Reasoning with her or comforting her won't be enough. One effective way to distract her from hunger is through play. Play actually takes our attention away from instinctual urges.

Play has deep, evolutionary roots; is present across all cultures and many species; and is deeper than gender. Scientists believe that even dinosaurs played with bones.[3] By play, we mean the ability to immerse yourself in some activity that you deeply enjoy to the point that you get caught up in the moment, suspend judgment, and allow yourself to have a good time. It can be something as simple as reading your favorite comic book, playing a sport, or trying out a new recipe if you like to cook. Like most of us, you probably take life too seriously, but the very good news is that it's not too late for any of us. We are hardwired for play, and we have a lifelong ability to enjoy it.

Dr. Stuart Brown, the founder of the National Institute for Play, explains that play is crucial for our neurological and personality development.[4] People whose childhoods were play-deprived experience lasting deficits across a range of intellectual, emotional, and interpersonal measures. On the flip side, species of animal that are more naturally playful, such as crows, dolphins, and chimpanzees, also show higher forms of cognitive intelligence and problem-solving abilities, which suggests a direct correlation between the two. Play makes us more open to possibilities, more trusting of our circumstances, more optimistic, and therefore more adaptable to change and more likely to improvise—making success and innovation far more likely than they ever could be in an atmosphere of grinding unhappiness and pessimism. It unleashes and bolsters our creative abilities, as evidenced by brain-imaging scans, shifting us out of the Square approach into imagination, artistry, and scientific ingenuity. Play also improves our attention span, reliability, and productivity. After years of research, Dr. Brown concluded that "Play is no less important than oxygen. It's a powerful force of nature that is essential to the very survival of the human race."

While most of us were taught at school to do your homework first and play later, it turns out that blending play with work can actually help you make fewer mistakes! If you feel stuck, or are procrastinating and not motivated to take action, ask your smartphone device to play your favorite movie soundtrack and start singing and dancing. If you start moving your body, you'll reap its energy, and you'll feel it immediately. But if you don't move, if you keep fighting for concentration, it will be like swimming against the tide. You will become more tired, more frustrated, and increasingly less productive. Therefore, while structure, logic, and analysis are clearly important, they should never stand in the way of our primal instinct to play, and in fact can even be enhanced by it.[5]

Here are three recommendations we offer our clients to help them incorporate play into work.

- Allocate regular time in which employees are explicitly encouraged to play, and provide games like LEGO Serious Play. This particular game's methodology combines visual, auditory, and kinesthetic learning styles into one uniquely creative and powerful approach. It teaches people with either a Square or Circle preference to think with their hands and better communicate their ideas, facilitating a greater flow of information.

- Share the SQUIRCLE Game with their employees and explain how it will help them progressively shift from an analytical, controlling approach to situations to a more intuitive one, thereby enabling them to better tap into their problem-solving skills, overcome even the most complex challenges, and form powerful synergies between the most diverse team members.

- Create or give employees access to physical spaces that are conducive to play. A great example of this is the Pixar campus in Emeryville, California, which has giant sculptures to encourage people to think big; human-size movie characters to bring out the child in employees' minds; a music festival to inspire employees and their families; and offices personally decorated by employees, who are encouraged to do so.[6] Another good example is plumbing-products manufacturer Kohler Company in Sheboygan, Wisconsin, which has an artist's residency program.[7] Employees can interact with the artists in residence for a creativity boost and for personal recreation.

- Give employees implicit and explicit permission to "fail" or be "unproductive" in their pursuit of innovation or business performance. Take the Spanish fast-fashion company Mango. With 2,100 stores in 110 countries, supply chain and logistics require highly dependable processes (Square). Yet the company explicitly promotes the "practice of a culture of mistakes" (Circle) in its written policies. Minnesota's global company 3M is well known for the invention of the Post-it Note, which was born out of the free time it gives to its employees. Workers are allowed to devote 20 percent of their normal work hours to what the company calls "unproductive time," and one employee pursued choral singing as a hobby. This was when he had the genius idea for a sticky piece of paper that he could use to mark pages in his musical score.

The results of a study published by Scientific American Mind showed that surgeons who play video games during their downtime make "one-third fewer errors in the operating room" than surgeons who don't and that "video games can improve dexterity, while boosting eye coordination, depth perception and pattern recognition."[8] It goes on to say that people who play video games for a few hours a week have better attention spans and information-processing skills than nongamers, and when nongamers spend a week playing video games, their visual perception skills improve. It also concluded that white-collar professionals who play video games are more confident and social.

Ways to Play

• Walk your dog • Swap riddles with an upbeat friend • Ask your kids silly questions • Play a word game on your phone • In your mind, come up with the worst solution to the problem you're solving • Start thinking about your Halloween costume • Play your favorite video game • Book a family activity in a Virtual Reality space • Sign up for a cooking class in your neighborhood • Play LEGOs with your kids • Plant flowers in your garden • Build a sandcastle on the beach or a snowman in the park during the winter • Do arts and crafts with old boxes, cans, plastics, and used gift wrap • Assemble a collage with cutouts from old magazines • Play the SQUIRCLE Game with your family members, friends, or colleagues

---

3. How well you tolerate uncertainty. Your ability to deal with the unknown, to pivot when taken by surprise, or to tolerate ambiguity is an essential skill. In life, as in nature, there are no straight lines and there is no way to ever be 100 percent sure of everything. This is why a level of tolerance for confusion is very instrumental. For example, a 2017 study by the National Institutes of Health (NIH) showed that the ability of physicians to tolerate ambiguity and uncertainty is proven to have a great impact on their clinical practice and may also lower their stress levels.[9] In contrast, the same study showed that a lower degree of tolerance for ambiguity and a higher need for cognitive closure predicted higher levels of work-related stress. In a previous NIH study, intolerance for uncertainty was even linked to anxiety and depression.[10]

For all of us, at least one thing *is* certain: things will change. It may be an unsettling fact, but it's one you can count on. So how can we get comfortable with the ambiguous and the unknown? Start by reflecting on how you have reacted in the past when something unexpected happened. How did you respond to the new situation? What was your emotional state? How did your reaction compare to how you have felt in other ambiguous situations? Thinking back to how you've handled previous surprises and disruptions will give you a good indication of your general tolerance for confusion.

How can you get better at it? Here are a few tips.

- Talk to friends, family members, or colleagues about how they felt in similar situations. Realizing that we share the same human fears and emotions with others is reassuring.

- Ask these same people to evaluate their own level of tolerance for uncertainty using a scale from one to ten. Once you understand their tendencies and inclinations, you will be better prepared to listen to or work with them. Their perspectives and subjective experiences will also be more acceptable and instructive to you.

- When you are faced with a problem that is plagued by ambiguity, establish what you know and what you don't. If you are part of a team, you should do this in a group. You will find that, often, people are not confused by the same aspects of a situation, but by different ones. This process can help clarify if not the full picture, at least a bigger part of the picture than you would have been able to clarify alone.

- Develop multiple action plans that correspond to different scenarios. This will help you move away from overreacting.

- Experiment. Try things that you have never tried before— even if it's a minor thing like the way you delegate certain tasks, changing how meetings are organized, or what time of day you allow your kids to play in the backyard—and see how this bit of spontaneity affects your feelings about the uncertain situation you're trying to resolve. Experimentation is the only path through the unknown. It's true for all of us, even those who are not scientists.

- Come to a resolution about a first step. Even in total darkness, we still have to make one first step forward if any progress is to be made. Movement creates energy; new perspectives and possibilities will emerge.

Now, to complement your Circle mindset, here are three proven measures of a well-developed Square approach.

1. How well you collect and analyze facts when making a decision. Information helps you to better evaluate your options, inform your process, and ground your choices in reality. However, we need to remember that even when we are focusing on data and logic, we may still be influenced by cognitive biases that distort our thinking, affect our beliefs, and sway the decisions and judgments we make every day. The most frequent one is probably *confirmation bias*, in which people tend to favor or pay more attention to information that confirms their previously held beliefs. Other biases include *anchoring*, in which people weigh one piece of information too heavily when making decisions, and *loss aversion*, which makes them too cautious.[11] It is important to be aware of these biases so that they don't lead you astray. A 2010 McKinsey study of more than one thousand major business investments showed that when organizations worked at reducing bias in their decision-making processes, they achieved returns up to 7 percentage points higher.[12]

So how can you put this into practice? The first step is to become aware that reducing biases makes a difference. Here are three other steps to ensure that you are using reason and data productively:

- Review the relevant facts, and always be sure that you get them from people who know more about the details than you do;

- Figure out if anyone making the recommendation to you or for you is intentionally clouding the facts in some way;

- Apply your own personal experience, knowledge, and reasoning to decide whether the recommendation is right.

Naturally, it is challenging to recognize our own cognitive biases. Even if we do, it may not be enough because we tend to accept our own biases and are often unable to eliminate them. This is why, for important decisions, you need to critically examine not only your information but also your process, and discuss them with others, preferably someone who has a SQUIRCLE profile different from yours. They can potentially help you see where biases may have steered you off track.

Why It's Hard to Avoid Biases

In a 2011 article from the Harvard Business Review, cognitive scientists concluded that there are two modes of thinking: System One and System Two.[13] System One uses intentions, impressions, associations, feelings, and preparations to produce actions and reactions that flow effortlessly. System One's view of the world is constant, and it allows us to do things like take a walk, avoid obstacles in our path, and contemplate something else all at the same time, or to feel sadness when we watch an emotional scene in a movie. We're in this mode when we brush our teeth, banter with friends, or drive our car on a long, straight interstate highway. We're not consciously focusing on how to do those things; we just do them. In contrast, System Two thinking is slow, effortful, and deliberate. This mode is at work when we complete a tax form, study a textbook, or learn to drive. Both modes are continuously active, but System One monitors things based on previous information and experience while System Two is mobilized when the stakes are high, when we detect an obvious error, or when original, rule-based reasoning is required. Most of the time System One determines our thoughts. Because System One is so good at adapting without us being aware of its operations, it can lead us astray. The stories it creates are generally accurate, but there are exceptions, including cognitive biases. One insidious feature of these cognitive failures is that we have no way of knowing that they're happening; we almost never catch ourselves in the act of making one because experience doesn't help us recognize them. (However, if we tackle a difficult problem using System Two thinking and fail to solve it, we're uncomfortably aware of that fact.)

This inability to sense that we've made a mistake is the key to understanding why we generally accept our first, most effortless conclusions or thinking at face value. It also explains why, even when we're aware of the existence of biases, we're not excited about eliminating them in ourselves. After all, it's difficult for us to fix errors that we can't see.

This is where people with a Square profile can play a big role. Because they lean toward hard facts and analytical reasoning, they can be instrumental in challenging the assumptions and process of Circle and Square profiles alike. Even if a Square is unaware of their own biases, they will be able to spot them in others. The advent of big data is extremely helpful in terms of fact-finding, identifying benchmarks, and gaining new perspectives (Square), but we still have the ultimate responsibility to be subjective (Circle) and draw the right conclusions (SQUIRCLE). This is why we all need to work toward a strong synergy between Square and Circle approaches.

2. How well you are able to organize—whatever "organize" means to you—the environment in which you live and operate. We all live and function in a specific environment, at home and at work, made up of physical space and people, and shaped by culture. Whether a person works in an office or from home, their environment directly influences their well-being, work performance, and productivity. A Procedia Engineering study about the influence of physical office environments on employees concluded that a comfortable working environment is important and enables employees to focus and do their best.[14] In short, a more pleasant environment and improved quality of life at work lead to better organizational performance all around. Another study released by Wiley Publishing in 2011, based on data collected from 274 knowledge workers in twenty-seven small and medium-size companies, showed that both the social-organizational work environment and the physical space independently affected creative performance. Therefore, if you want to be more successful and boost levels of on-the-job or at-home happiness and fulfillment, establishing an environment that is attuned to your personal needs and preferences is a must. A Square's natural capacity to assess information, organize, and formulate practical solutions is a tremendous asset in this regard. They have an innate tendency to create systems and routines that make their lives easier and to put structures in place to help themselves and others get things done.

The tricky part, however, is that we're all unique, and as soon as we interact with other people in a constant, enduring way (whether in a marriage, a business partnership, or a shared office) we have to contend with their needs and wants. When organizing your environment, you have to plan according to what works for you as well as what is compatible with those who are living or working alongside you. If you don't have a firm grasp on your own personal preferences, you may be swayed from what works best for you, so making choices that will optimize a shared work environment requires clarity of mind, discernment, assertiveness, and determination (Square). Here are three simple tips to help you construct a space that works for all.

- Get to know the SQUIRCLE profile of your partners and colleagues both at home and at work. Doing so will help you formulate a plan that takes both Square and Circle preferences and expectations regarding environment into account, and will enable you to cohabitate more easily. This type of due diligence and time investment (Square) will pay off.

- If you require different kinds of stimulation, whether through physical activity or interaction with others, decide where and how they will happen and make them a part of your daily routine. On the other hand, if you need solitude and stillness, make sure that you have the space and means to protect those as well. Either way, you will need to put them down in your schedule as must-haves that cannot be set aside for meetings or other obligations. This will require honest self-assessment, planning, and discipline (Square).

- Reflect on your organizing system, make it personal, and implement it. We've all heard of people who organize the clothes in their wardrobe by color or fabric type just because it looks beautiful while others organize their closets to optimize space and functionality. Likewise, some people alphabetize the spices in the kitchen cabinet while others keep the spices that they use most at the front of the shelf and the ones they use less frequently in the back. Don't underestimate the increased utility or peace of mind that can come with a personalized system designed for you *by* you; devoting some time to finding out what works best will make your life easier and free up brainpower for other activities.

3. How well you are able to tap into your network and the resources it offers. We cannot get very far in life without cooperating with others, so the ability to mobilize the people around you is paramount if you want to achieve your goals. Yet when you're the rainmaker at home, work, or both, it's hard to imagine that someone else can do it for you. Many of us have trouble reaching out for help and support. Asking for help chips away at our self-esteem. We don't like to appear weak or feel dependent on others when, in fact, it's an integral part of resource management (Square) that is very effective. You need to systematically look at your environment as if it were a chessboard and make the best use of the allies around you.

• The Great Work Study conducted by the O.C. Tanner Institute in 2017 shows that asking for advice or even merely support helps people to be more successful in life.[15] The study revealed that 72 percent of people who receive awards for their work regularly ask for advice and opinions from people outside their inner circle. It seems that asking for help and advice actually produces better, stronger, more successful results, and helps you protect your greatest asset—yourself—from taking on too much, bearing too heavy a load of responsibility, and potential burnout.

In seminars, when the time comes for participants to discuss how to implement the innovative solutions they have designed, we help them build very detailed action plans. As part of those plans, we ask them to carefully identify the people in the organization who will be either assistors or resistors to change. This is a perfect example of assessing your chessboard and the network that surrounds you. Participants can then come up with strategies and tactics to utilize their assistors and work around resistors during implementation.

There is also empirical evidence, as seen in organizations like Weight Watchers or Alcoholics Anonymous, that choosing to be part of a community you can trust and share with is key to overcoming challenges and reaching your goals. Surrounding ourselves with people who accept us for who we are and who understand our particular needs and wants, who are willing to listen to our experiences and share their own, makes us more human, more willing to change and grow. Here are three suggestions to help you rethink reaching for help:

- Consider asking others for their expertise and insights as a way to gain data (Square) through new perspectives;
- Think of asking for advice as a sign of acknowledgment (Square) for those around you;
- Imagine that asking for help shows others that you are brave enough to commit (Square) to getting out of your comfort zone and that you are able to responsibly maneuver through difficult situations by seeking guidance.[16]

These six measures are an excellent starting point, but how can you perfect your SQUIRCLE attitude? You'll find answers to this question and more practical tips at www.squircleacademy.com. Simply download the "SQUIRCLE You" course on one of your devices to learn how to achieve a perfect synergy between the Square and Circle aspects of your personality!

QUESTIONS

- Can you recall a time when you felt overwhelmed by an emotion? Did you notice any sensations in your body?
- What are your favorite ways to play to engage your creative spirit?
- How chaotic is your family life? Does that make you excited or frustrated? How might you accept the chaos of it?
- Have you ever been in a situation where you called out someone on their confirmation bias?
- How is your personal system of organization? Have you given it a lot of thought? If yes, how does it work for the people around you?
- How hard is it for you to ask for help? Have you ever considered it to be a sign of strength in others, if not in you?

SQUIRCLE
& Others

If you want to go fast, go alone. If you want to
go far, go together.

—AFRICAN PROVERB

I never knew anybody . . . who found life simple. I
think a life or a time looks simple when you leave out
the details.

—URSULA K. LE GUIN

Whatever your SQUIRCLE profile might be, you will always need to collaborate with people of all types because we cannot go very far in life alone. When people who are different from each other in terms of nationality, physical appearance, religion, education, age, gender, or sexual orientation join together at work or in their personal lives, this provides a variety of points of view, whether from a social, cultural, or personal standpoint. Today, it is a well-researched fact that diversity is a driver of prosperity,[1] and brings innovation[2] and adaptation[3] to the areas of human science, business, and the economy, all of which are necessary to thrive in today's global world.

Communication and how we interact with others are at the heart of any collaboration. In Carl Jung's theory of psychological types, the biggest source of discord in any relationship is the difference in the way we individually process information.[4] A Square approach looks at concrete facts and analyzes them; a Circle approach will want to focus on the big picture, its deeper meaning, and the realm of possibilities that it offers. Perceptions don't match and desired outcomes can be polar opposites. Therefore, the cause of frustration is real.

Let's say that you are planning for a weekend outing with your spouse. The Square approach would be to solidify your itinerary, timing, and hotel reservation, all the way down to the perfect picnic basket and a plan to fill up the car the night before departure. In contrast, the Circle approach is to be excited about all the possibilities the trip might bring and to leave their options open when it comes to the itinerary, hotel room, or even the departure time. Who knows? Something great might happen that morning that you don't want to miss!

These divergent approaches might seem a bit exaggerated, but they represent two clear orientations. If you are in a situation in which you need to collaborate with someone who has a different SQUIRCLE profile, you have two options. You can choose to focus on the differences and see them as problematic, but looking at them in this way will only result in a tug-of-war. Or you can see them as complementary and draw on both profiles to make everything happen in a fairly reliable way while still leaving room for flexibility and surprises. The most challenging part will be the planning phase because the Square profile will need reassurance that the details are taken care of and will feel unsettled if they are not. For the Circle profile, there will probably be some impatience about the need to discuss so many details ahead of time because, from a Circle perspective, they can be figured out as the trip unfolds.

Now imagine planning this same trip in an environment in which there are a lot of unknowns. Let's say that the weather seems rather unpredictable due to a potential snowstorm. Which approach do you think would be best suited to adapt to the lack of certainty? A Square would probably prefer to cancel for the sake of caution, regardless of their disappointment over the missed opportunities that come from forgoing a great weekend away. A Circle would probably stay open to the possibility of a great adventure, which the Square might see as being irresponsible, although it's not meant to be. Of course, there are many other factors to be taken into account, such as the cancellation policy of the hotel and the reliability of the car in severe weather. There is no right or wrong decision here; it's purely a matter of personal preference. However, the situation is complex because it faces off two sets of subjective preferences and expectations, and there will need to be awareness and compromise to come up with a plan that everyone feels good about.

We live in a more and more unpredictable world, and the pace of disruption is only accelerating. Today's innovations are coming out of left field, leveraging technology to cater to consumer lifestyles and offer a better value proposition, whether they're about transforming the way we buy food; hire car services; access news, information, or entertainment; or protect ourselves from viral epidemics. It is clear that a Circle approach allows for more options, possibilities, and flexible adaptation in a VUCA (Volatile, Unknown, Complex, and Ambiguous) world. A Square approach will provide cautionary self-checks and careful scenario planning. However, planning alone will not be enough. As in the SQUIRCLE Game, everything in life is constantly in flux and no one knows where the next move will come from, so whether your preference is for Circle or Square, it is important to acknowledge the essential unpredictability of any situation, including when two different profiles communicate! The Square needs to value the Circle's ability to adapt to the unknown, and the Circle needs to be mindful of presenting new plans in a factual and thoughtful manner that can be fully appreciated by the Square. Circle types often suffer unfairly in interpersonal communications because of our culture's Square bias. Their views are often overlooked, sometimes criticized, and rarely taken seriously. As a result, we often miss our chance to gain an edge or a competitive advantage in identifying new solutions and opportunities. It's hard for the Circle, but it's also hard for the Square, who wants to minimize risk and make the most informed decisions possible.

Here is a typical dialogue between Alex and Jo, who work together in the baby beverage division of a food company.

Jo: When I look back at the opportunity that we missed last year, I feel strongly that there's another big chance for us here this spring. I feel we should relaunch our new kids' super smoothie with a slightly different tagline that speaks more to the current mindset of parents and the latest health trends emerging in this category.

Alex: It sounds interesting. Tell me more about the facts that led you to this supposition.

Jo: It's not about facts; it's about what I've personally observed in stores and on websites that cater to young parents and what I've gleaned from talking to my moms' group and other friends who have kids.

Alex: I hear you, Jo. All right, let's dig deeper and analyze the market data and evaluate precisely the size of the opportunity before we take that kind of risk and rebrand.

Jo: Given the usual speed of our internal processes, by the time we're done with this type of analysis, it might well be too late for us to pivot and react.

Alex: So let's start now and try to make some quick progress in determining whether there's actually evidence for what you are saying. We'll reevaluate once we can rely on a few hard facts.

Jo: [who knows they will likely miss the window of opportunity] Oh well.

So how do we see eye to eye? As a Square, remember that sometimes in the name of logic we run the risk of becoming illogical. Why? Because we apply a binary model (good/bad, facts/possibilities, reasonable/unreasonable) to life situations that are rarely binary. Let's take the example of college education. Students have to pass an exam, or they will fail. In this case, studying revolves around accumulating knowledge or skills in order to meet a certain set of criteria. Students are set up in a binary system—right versus wrong—which automatically narrows the scope of their experience while pursuing a degree. This obviously doesn't fully match the larger purpose of higher education, which is to lead a happier and more fruitful life with a greater awareness of oneself, society, and the world. So it's important for a Square to make an effort to open up to what Circle profiles have to say. You don't have to agree with them; simply step back, pause, and truly listen in a receptive way, as participants do in the SQUIRCLE Game. When you do this, you give yourself a chance to leave behind the black-and-white screen and see the situation in full color. The Circle approach might feel more complicated at first, but it's not. As we have seen, you need to embrace and welcome the complexity of any scenario for truly creative solutions to emerge.

To this point, it's important to clarify the difference between complication and complexity. In his book, *Reinventing Organizations*, Frederic Laloux explains it very well through two examples. First, he talks about a Boeing aircraft, which he describes as a complicated system; although there are tens of thousands of components to it, they come together following a linear logic. If you were to pull out any single piece and give it to an engineer, they would be able to tell you whether the missing piece has an impact on the functioning of the aircraft, and if yes, which one. Second, Laloux gives the example of a plate of spaghetti as a complex system. It contains only a dozen ingredients, but if you pull on a single noodle, no computer, even the most powerful one in the world, will be able to predict exactly what will happen.

Human interactions are complex. There is no manual to help us master relationships. There are tools, but they'll never be enough, and they can never account for all the different variables and the remarkable spontaneity of human thought and emotion. Like Emma, the girl who with the best of intentions confuses the cage with the parrot's nest, Squares can make a similar error if they mistake tools for human experience and trade a desire to learn and grow for a desire to control.

As a Circle, understand that your Square counterpart is wearing a different pair of lenses than you are, and try to imagine what it would be like for you to see life in black and white, in terms of concretes and absolutes. You'll likely have more empathy for the Square profile and why it is sometimes hard for them to picture the colors you're referring to. Be open to your differences and the richness they can bring to your interactions. By paying more attention to facts and logical reasoning, Squares can bring objectivity, planning, reliability, and timeliness to your collaborations—all positive factors that help people avoid mistakes due to an excess of enthusiasm, a lack of attention to detail, or both. You will start valuing what you might have first perceived as limits to your creative ideas and realize that planning can, on the contrary, give you peace of mind and space for ideation and creative activities. Additionally, the more you acquaint yourself with Square qualities, the more likely you are to be in a position to deconstruct the traditional Square approach and introduce nonrational aspects into the conversation. Breakthroughs in communication are possible if you invite the Square profile into the "nonrational" space by explaining that there is more to the situation than can be rationally understood, as in the following scenario.

Cameron: My son Dylan did well in junior high; he was in the top one percent of his class, but now, in high school, he's struggling. The school has a fantastic reputation, it ranks high statewide and even nationally, but ever since he enrolled there, his grades have been consistently less than average. I don't understand what's happening.

Ezra: Really?

Cameron: Yes! Two months ago, I even hired a tutor the school had recommended to me as one of the best. The tutor helps him with his homework each day after school, but it hasn't helped.

Ezra: How does Dylan feel about it?

Cameron: I don't think he values or appreciates the opportunity he has to be a part of such an excellent educational system. It's a shame! He'll regret it one day.

Ezra: Are you sure he really feels that way?

Cameron: He doesn't listen when I talk to him about his grades. He doesn't seem to even care.

Ezra: What do you feel the problem is?

Cameron: I don't know. I wonder if I should find another school for him.

Ezra: How do you feel about the situation?

Cameron: I think I need to find a solution sooner rather than later because I feel certain that it's only going to get worse.

Ezra: Cameron, I remember how much he loved all his activities in junior high school: guitar, sports, robotics. He was able to play sports or rehearse with his band almost every day after school and still get great marks. That's something about him that always amazed me. Have you sat down with Dylan to ask him how he feels about school and whether he enjoys what he's learning and studying?

Cameron: No, I haven't. I just don't understand how, given his strong academic abilities, he's not able to be motivated, focused, and get results.

Ezra: I see a disconnect between your expectations and what is really happening at school. I think there must be something about his experience that he is not telling you. I feel like you owe him and yourself a real heart-to-heart conversation to try to get to a deeper understanding of the situation. Obviously pushing him harder has not worked. It's time to try something else.

Cameron: You're probably right. All the logical remedies have not worked. What do you think I should say?

Ezra: Why don't we experiment and role-play the

conversation you would like to have with him? Let's be open, start with sharing your feelings rather than thoughts, and see what unfolds . . .

Cameron initially uses a Square thought process to try to find a solution to the situation, but Ezra intuits (Circle) that Dylan's situation is more complex (Circle) than simply being a matter of applying himself and working harder (Square). Ezra attempts to get Cameron to share feelings rather than thoughts, but he uses a deductive process (Square) to help Cameron realize that it is time to change his course of action.

It has been my observation over the years that Circle profiles are less common than Squares. For this reason, Circles definitely bring diversity to the workplace and offer interesting alternative perspectives. However, I have also observed that when organizations begin a process of transformation, the biggest resistance to change often comes from the Circles, at least at first. This is because their relationship to their work is more emotional and value-based than it is for the Squares, who tend to be more rational and objective. Therefore the Square types usually have less personal attachment to the status quo, even if they may have more difficulty envisioning the future. As a result, we can clearly see why it is both a challenge and an opportunity for Square and Circle to collaborate.

We all have both Square and Circle tendencies within us, so this is not about pitting the population of Squares against the tribe of Circles. Under certain circumstances, a Circle profile can adopt a Square approach and vice versa. The one thing we know is that today, more than ever, it is imperative to make much more room for a Circle approach in terms of the way we interact and communicate, regardless of our profile.

This is especially important when similar profiles group together. Squares need to remember that they might miss a whole part of the picture when they communicate solely with each other. On the other hand, Circles working together need to understand that they might miss crucial Square steps in their thinking and creative processes due to their tendency to see only the big picture. The Square provides the critical baseline from which we can best experience and improvise in life, like the nest of the parrot, which allows it to come and go freely in the wilderness. Squares and Circles who enjoy fluency in both approaches can more easily express their own qualities and views, facilitating better communication and cooperation and helping each other overcome their blind spots.

If you are a Circle talking to a Square, consider these conversation starters:

- Before I share my ideas, why don't we start by reviewing the production budget?

- Let me first share three key facts that I extracted from the annual report.

- Before we get to the creative work, rest assured that we are totally on track with our timeline.

- I made plans to leave work early so I could arrive thirty minutes before our meeting.

- Honey, I want you to know that every day you were away, the kids were asleep before bedtime.

- For my next vacation, I have carefully organized who will cover for me on each project.

If you're a Square talking to a Circle, you might consider the following openers:

- What might help you reflect on these three defining facts?

- Let me first ask, how do you feel right now?

- What did you envision in terms of solutions after you read the monthly sales report?

- Would it be helpful to imagine a few creative scenarios before we dive into the report?

- What's the big picture here for you?

- Imagine that we're together five years from now. What would your ideal life with me be?

SQUARE Catchphrases

Here's the plan . . .

We must make sure we meet the deadline.

What are all the deliverables?

It has to be . . .

I can finance that . . .

Dinner is at six o'clock.

On the way home, pick up enough milk for breakfast for the entire week.

It's so complex! I can't wrap my mind around it.

Can someone show me the facts?

Let's understand the exact situation first.

Let's complete this first step before we think about the next one.

What is our timeline here?

Let's leave enough time to reach the airport at least three hours before departure.

CIRCLE Catchphrases

What if . . .

I feel . . .

Yes, and . . .

Can we . . .

Imagine . . .

In what ways might we . . .

I'll be home later.

Oh, that meeting is today?

Wow! It's beautifully complex and filled with so many possibilities.

Tell me more. I love this theory.

Great! The sky is the limit here.

Let's make the impossible possible.

Stop! Let's breathe for a minute . . .

Whatever your profile, you can go to www.squircleacademy.com and download our course, SQUIRCLE Collaboration, onto your device. There you will find more exercises and guidelines to help you best collaborate with all types at work and at home.

QUESTIONS

- What communication issues have arisen within your teams at work? Thinking about SQUIRCLE, how might you resolve them differently?
- How does it feel when you and a family member get "on the same wavelength," even though you might have different SQUIRCLE preferences?

10

SQUIRCLE
& Time

Punctuality is the thief of time.

— OSCAR WILDE

Above all don't fear difficult moments.
The best comes from them.

— RITA LEVI-MONTALCINI

We live in a high-speed world, where digital interconnection, sophisticated technology, and social media purportedly make us smarter, faster, and more effective. But greater digitization is also causing acute isolation; our connection to other humans and to nature is quietly being replaced by "fear of missing out" (FOMO) and social media angst.[1] In the workplace, burnout caused by chronic stress is widespread. The situation is so far reaching in developed countries that the World Health Organization has added "burnout" to its list of globally recognized diseases. They define it as a syndrome of "chronic workplace stress that has not been successfully managed," which includes "feelings of energy depletion or exhaustion" and results in "increased mental distance from one's job" and "reduced professional efficacy." Days seem to go by faster and the load of information to absorb is always bigger. Based on all the data, it's getting worse, yet we don't seem to be able to curb this trend. In a world that's more open, more connected, and more informed, we also aspire to more, whether that means more opportunities, productivity, or free time to travel the world. Yet our days are not any longer. All of us feel this time crunch, but it's hard to imagine a logical solution because the equation is rather impossible to solve: more commitments and obligations, all at an ever-increasing pace, within the same number of hours in the day. I call this situation the **Modern Time Conundrum (MTC)**.

MTC = (more things to do + more desire to do more + at a faster pace) / the same number of hours in the day

Something has to change. But what? My observation is that there is a fundamental misunderstanding of time. **Not every minute is equal,** and time is not always what we think it is. There is *external time.* For example, school starts at eight o'clock for my kids. I need to leave my house at 7:20 a.m. to be able to drop them off by 7:55 a.m. at the latest. Then there is *internal time,* as in, "Tonight I will eat later than usual because I had a late lunch. I will eat when I feel hungry." One kind is set, defined, imposed by a social convention. It is a human invention based on clocks and calendars. It's practical. It allows us to be in tempo with one another. We arrive before the store closes and on time to catch a movie before it starts.

As such, external time can also be thought of as Square time. And then there is the summer day we spend by the lake that feels as though it goes by in a few hours or the minutes we spend anxiously waiting for the result of a biopsy or a college entrance exam. Those minutes usually feel like an eternity. That time is subjective. It is visceral. It unspools inside of us. It is natural. **Therefore, internal time is also called Circle time.**

In our world, we will never be able to solve the MTC without taking into account Circle time. As with any other complex scenario, to solve MTC we need to approach the situation through a Circle mindset. **We need to start with nature.** It is because we dismiss nature in our relationship to time that burnout happens. If we were able to say the word "enough"— enough information, enough Instagram posts, enough travel commitments, enough meetings scheduled, or enough minutes spent checking emails—there would be no burnout. But we don't, and that's why burnout keeps spreading like a bad cold. We approach productivity and time management as if we are machines, but we're not mechanical, we're humans. We're not merely Square; we're Circle first. We have feelings, and they shape our thoughts. Yes, we invented the Square to function better, but we live in and are a part of nature, which is not Square. To curb burnout and live better lives we have to put on our Circle lens.

The problem today is not how *much* time you have; it is how *present* you are to the moment during that time.

Next we will go over the practical ways in which you can do this. First, let's talk about how to structure your day. Schedules and to-do lists are great, but they're only tools. A tool is designed to make your life easier, but *you* are in charge of time management. Your to-do list is not in charge. You have the capacity to make decisions about the use of your time, rather than simply doing things because they're on your list. Your schedule and to-do list are written in conventional Square time: forty-five minutes for this call, an hour for that meeting, an hour to make dinner, and so on. Effective time management that improves your performance *and* your well-being is first and foremost about Circle time. How do you *feel* about this forty-five-minute call? Could it be handled by email? Or could it be only fifteen minutes? How do you truly *feel* about the hours you spend on social media? Do they make you happier, or do they leave you feeling down? How do you *feel* about spending an hour making dinner when you could order out and play a game with your kids instead? **You can manage a lot of your time commitments if you take the extra step and think about how each to-do list item actually makes you feel and what you can do to mitigate these negative feelings.**

Instead of:	Try:
Sending multiple emails	*Picking up the phone or making plans with someone to talk in person*
Making many phone calls	*Conference call/video*
Making dinner	*Ordering out*
Social Media	*Calling a friend*
Status meetings	*Status report emails*
Lunch at your desk	*Have a protein shake and take a walk*
Compulsively checking your email	*Taking five deep breaths*

Some will probably say that is unrealistic to address your to-do list in terms of feelings because if your boss calls you into a one-hour meeting, you have little or no choice but to attend. But let's look now at the reality of time management at work. Here are a few facts. According to a McKinsey analysis, the average professional spends 28 percent of their workday reading and answering email.[2] For the typical full-time worker in America, that amounts to a staggering 2.6 hours spent on emails and 209 messages received every day.[3] However, a subsequent *Harvard Business Review* article showed that we can decrease the time we spend on email by approximately 50 percent by using research-backed time management practices to reduce email-processing time, saving one hour and twenty-one minutes without sacrificing effectiveness. They concluded that twenty-one minutes are wasted each day due to checking email too often.[4] On average, people check their email fifteen times a day, or every thirty-seven minutes. The solution consists of turning off notifications and scheduling time (about five to eight minutes) every hour to check email.

- Twenty-seven minutes are wasted due to full in-boxes that distract us into rereading old emails over and over again.

  The antidote is the single-touch rule, which is to systematically either keep aside or delete an email the first time you read it to avoid looking at it a second time.

- Fourteen minutes are wasted looking for older emails.

  To save these fourteen minutes, use a keyword search and integrate your emails with a to-do list app that automatically sorts your emails by task.

- Eleven minutes are wasted archiving emails into many folders using a mouse or trackpad.

  Research shows that you only need two folders: Follow-Up

(for emails that require a response or further action) and Read (for emails that contain important information we wish to read at a later time).

- Eight minutes are wasted reading and processing irrelevant emails. Sixty-two percent of all emails are unimportant and can be processed or deleted in bulk. Set up automated filtering of newsletters you want to keep, unsubscribe from those you don't, and block spam for unwanted emails that keep coming in spite of unsubscribing.

How to Make Email an Effective Tool Again[5]

- *Turn off notifications and instead check your email hourly*

- *Move every email out of your inbox the first time you read it*

- *Use the search functionality with search operators to find emails again*

- *Set up just two email folders, one for follow-up and one for read emails, and use shortcuts to archive emails there*

- *Avoid processing irrelevant or less important emails individually*

These habits and tips will help you save Square time in your day, which will directly allow you to achieve more. But equally important, you must set aside Circle time for yourself. This means time when you are physically and emotionally present rather than running on autopilot, focusing only on achievement and pushing yourself to complete tasks and make it through the day. As we saw with Emma and the parrot, Square time is a tool that we invented, but you can never let it become a prison for your Circle time. You need time in which you can feel, be spontaneous, and let your imagination be in a state of flow—not because you expect your imagination to produce but simply because it needs free space in order for you to stay healthy and capable of forming true connections with others.

Practicing SQUIRCLE Time

If you're a Square profile, it's probably easy for you to manage to-do lists, but how often do you schedule Circle time in your day? Does your to-do list include time to check in with your body through deep breathing, physical exercise, or even a power nap? Can you plan to do one of these instead of checking your email once more or planning another meeting or task? Look at your past week and mark in red the scheduled windows of Square time both at home and at work, when your primary goal was about being efficient, results-oriented, and productive. Now mark in green the times in your day when you were able to be in the moment, even if it was for a work-related idea or a project that you contemplated with little expectation in terms of outcome. Then mark in green the time you set aside to do nothing but improvise according to whatever felt right in the moment. Now compare the red and green marks. Red marks show the moments when you are in an exploitative relationship with your body. Green marks are moments when you are in a regenerative relationship with your body. The proportion between red and green is a direct indication of how you spend your time and whether it reflects your professional and personal objectives. If you feel stressed out, rebalancing your schedule will help: you should make an effort to increase Circle time and reduce Square time. One simple solution is to reduce sixty-minute meetings to forty-five minutes and thirty-minute meetings to twenty minutes by asking every participant to come better prepared. You might also share and discuss your color-coded schedule with family members, friends, or colleagues to compare your individual results.

If you're a Circle profile, to-do lists might be harder for you. Either way, I would recommend that you honor your Circle preference in terms of your choice of tools for time management. Many Circle profiles appreciate the simple structure a to-do list offers so that they won't forget an important task or have no idea where their day might take them. Other Circle profiles forget to write one entirely or lose the list before the day is out. Figure out what puts the least stress on your body. Discuss with other Circle profiles and Even profiles how they go about managing their time and, more importantly, their satisfaction and enjoyment of life. The red-and-green-marker exercise above is helpful too.

However, the challenge for Circles is that when they're in the flow, their awareness of Square time vanishes. This is good because these moments of flow are helpful in terms of stress; Circles don't, for example, feel the pressure of a deadline. However, when they come out of their state of flow, they may realize they just spent two hours writing an email on which they had only planned to spend thirty minutes. This is where Squares can help them greatly to keep up with project timelines as they overcome procrastination.

University of Calgary professor Piers Steel states in his book, *The Procrastination Equation*, that putting off tasks is a human condition that is shared among 95 percent of us.[6] Procrastination, he believes, is a purely visceral reaction to something we don't want to do. The more averse you are to a task, the more likely you are to put it off. Steel asserts that the duties we procrastinate share one or more of the following characteristics; either they are: boring, frustrating, difficult, ambiguous, unstructured, not intrinsically rewarding (i.e., you don't find the process fun), or lacking in personal meaning. For Circles especially, setting these feelings aside and finding the motivation to get the job done can be a struggle.

This is where you need to be emotionally savvy (Circle) and disciplined (Square) in order to recognize and admit your emotional ambivalence about the project. Keep a log of when and what you procrastinate about so that you can evaluate the extent of the problem. The challenge then becomes doing something about it. You will need to take two simple but necessary steps, and even if you are a Circle, you cannot permit yourself to have feelings or second thoughts about either one. First, you have to commit to the task, and second, just do it. "On a neurological level, procrastination is not the slightest bit logical," writes Chris Bailey, author of *Hyperfocus: How to Be More Productive in a World of Distraction*,[7] in an article for the *Harvard Business Review*.[8] Once you've realized this, you have to step back and look at the task with an emotionally detached Square lens. You have to be surgical, get to know your triggers, and then remove feelings from the procrastination equation.

If this is still too daunting for a Circle, or if they cannot relate to this type of discipline, there is another creative way to do this, and that is to trick your mind by using your active imagination. This consists of coming up with an imaginary story that will entice you to overcome the aversion you felt before. For example, you can give the task an uplifting name—like "Love Task," "Labor of Love," or "Genius Project"—and make yourself the heroic protagonist of this story, with a name like "Professor Efficiency" or the "Wizard Do-It-All." Rather than staying seated in your chair thinking or worrying about your project, start moving to engage physically with the topic at hand and awaken energy and uproot your inertia. You can also use discipline to get started and then combine it with creative imagination along the way to keep yourself engaged through the completion of the task.

Whatever your profile, you can go to www.squircleacademy.com and download our course, SQUIRCLE Time, onto your device. There you will find more exercises and guidelines to help you overcome your MTC (Modern Time Conundrum).

QUESTİONS

- Yesterday, what tasks did you deal with that were Square tasks? Circle Tasks? How did you feel about the balance?
- How can you start to eliminate distractions and minimize interruptions in your workday and at home?

11

SQUIRCLE
Stories

Nothing gets transformed in your life until your mind is transformed.

—IFEANYI ENOCH ONUOHA

It always seems impossible until it is done.

—NELSON MANDELA

Meet Marie

"The world is screaming for new ways of thinking. The old way doesn't work anymore. I am happy I embraced a new attitude."

Nature of the Challenge:

Finding new momentum and motivation.

Situation:

In spite of notable professional success, Marie is struggling to find the motivation to promote her photographs and get them into the best museum collections around the world.

Context:

Marie, a French American, is a successful artistic photographer whose work has earned her international professional recognition. One of the peak moments in her career was a highly acclaimed solo exhibition at the Kennedy Center in Washington, DC. But when she attended our SQUIRCLE atelier, she confessed that she felt stuck when it came to promoting her work. As the former head of the South American office of a global photo agency, she'd had firsthand experience with a Square approach to business. Since quitting this executive job, she'd been enjoying a more relaxed, Circle approach to life, especially when diving into the creative process of photography. Now, however, she wanted to get her photographs into more museum collections so that she could better raise money for her next big project.

Process to Breakthrough:

In SQUIRCLE ateliers, participants work together in teams to help each other put SQUIRCLE to use. Lynn, another participant, helped Marie realize that she was operating as an artist with a free-flowing Circle mindset, but she was finding it hard to integrate a Square approach and be accountable to any defined goals or results beyond her general wish for success. Lynn, a married mother of two, is an independent consultant who is very organized and a master of to-do lists. She recommended that Marie commit (a Square action) to writing a letter to the curators at various museums and to do it the very next day, without any hesitation or waffling. But instead of adopting the businesslike tone that she'd used in her management days, Marie was to write spontaneously, from her heart (a Circle approach). This would provide the momentum she needed to get started and also allow the curators who read the letter to feel her passion for photography.

Marie followed Lynn's advice. The next day, she sent her draft to Lynn, who gave her positive feedback and told Marie that she thought many curators would be interested in getting to know more about her work. Marie kept the momentum going and emailed her letters immediately, without giving herself any time or space in which to doubt herself. Then something incredible happened. Marie received multiple responses via email, literally overnight.

Outcome:

As a result, Marie got her photographs into three world-renowned museums. The process of committing to both taking steps and writing from her heart was an inspiring and affirming experience for her, one that she cherishes and tries to replicate and build on every day in other areas of her life.

Lesson Learned: Square and Circle are interdependent and in fact produce the best results together. Using Square doesn't mean giving up Circle. Circle can actually make Square work for you. Your approach can retain its personal and creative signature, even if it is methodical and practical.

Meet Rebecka

*"The empowerment of women . . .
and men matters. We all need
to embrace more our creative sides."*

Nature of the Challenge:

Making space for creativity at work.

Situation:

Working in a fast-moving, high-tech environment,
Rebecka found it difficult to slow down to make space
for creativity in her life.

Context:

A young millennial from the Midwest, Rebecka is an
AI/data product manager. She has long struggled with
balancing linear and creative work. In the office, she's
constantly in a "do, do, do" mode. She feels severely
stressed out and longs for more emotional balance and
the ability to make space for her creative self, but she
has little idea of how to undo this cycle.

Process to Breakthrough:

By attending SQUIRCLE workshops and learning
about the power of breath (especially through the
SQUIRCLE Game), Rebecka began to understand how
to pause, both when she was alone and with others.
She also discovered new ways to be more emotionally

vulnerable, which made it easier for her to connect and communicate with colleagues. Her first step was to experiment with the way she was expressing herself at work. In meetings, she shifted from immediately jumping into the subject matter (a Square action) to first checking in with everyone around the table (a Circle approach). She noticed a resulting sense of relaxation in herself and in others that made running the meetings easier for her. She also realized that she was less tired coming out of those team sessions. At the same time, she decided to take regular breaks during the day whenever her body felt stiff from sitting or her ears were buzzing from long conference calls. These repeated short breaks allowed her to meet and bond with different people at the watercooler, and she was able to be more open and chat with them about personal fun stuff like their favorite Netflix shows or restaurants, something she would never have been able to do when sitting at her desk all day long. To be more physically active without reducing her working hours, she asked for an adjustable standing desk, which helped her posture and a lingering back pain from a yoga injury. She also made an effort to walk home from work more often.

Bit by bit, Rebecka saw her mood improve and her relationships with her colleagues deepen, a shift that she finds extremely valuable in business. Eventually, she was also more available to pursue her own creative aspirations. She began incorporating time for Circle activities into her schedule and would start these sessions with a minute of deep breathing followed by sensory focusing—that is, time for taking in her environment through each of her five senses. This made her less tense and often sparked interesting creative insights about where to look for inspiration or how to start working on a new idea.

Outcome:

Rebecka learned the power of pausing and vulnerability. Being in touch with her emotions made it easier to identify and commit to her priorities and to involve others along the way. She was able to progressively find space in her schedule to slow down and reflect, which in turn opened the natural gateway to her creativity. Today, she even has a "play/pause" tattoo on her right arm, a reminder of how her life has changed.

> **Lesson Learned: Tech is a very Square environment, but Rebecka knows she doesn't need to live exclusively in the Square at work.**

Meet Levon

"Who cares about fitting in a Square world that's less and less relevant?"

Nature of the challenge:

How to stay creative in an environment where there are more and more restrictions imposed on you.

Situation:

As Levon became more successful, more creative restrictions were put upon him that frustrated his need to be inventive and original and that took joy out of his daily life.

Context:

Levon, an American of Armenian descent, is a successful hairdresser and makeup artist. He enjoys a clientele of high net worth individuals, celebrities, and Hollywood stars, yet he found it harder and harder to express his creativity in a world where he felt limited and inhibited in his artistry due to increasing legal constraints, tedious financial negotiations, and the demanding whims of clients driven by short-lived trends on social media. One of his biggest challenges as a freelancer in high demand was to negotiate his fees when he was hired, sometimes for as long as an entire week, by a celebrity or socialite at a fashion show in Paris, Milan, or New York. He tended to be driven by creative enthusiasm (Circle) for the work rather than a sense of boundaries (Square) about his fees, his availability, or the insistent requests of his clients. This often made him feel resentful and frustrated during such intense trips.

Process to Breakthrough:

When Levon saw for the first time the image of the Circle squared in and trapped, he felt that it represented his struggle as a creative professional. It helped him understand why it was hard for him as a Circle to balance the rules of the Square with his creative aspirations. For him, "creativity is inspired by a desire to share with the world new, heartfelt possibilities." He considered his work an act of love, and as such he felt that it should be honored and retributed fairly and with care. But the people who hired him generally had a different viewpoint. As much as they enjoyed his talent, they still saw their relationship as a commercial transaction rather than one about emotional bonding. Through group discussions, he was able to shift his self-perception and rethink his responsibility in his client relationships. This in turn allowed him to approach his profession from a more practical standpoint (Square) and to take these difficult dynamics less personally. He was also able to envision how he could benefit from the Square in his professional life without giving into its systematic dominance: he could harness its power to set clear parameters and ask for fair compensation rather than being led solely by client wishes and his creative aspirations.

Outcome:

Ironically, when Levon allowed the Square to provide a framework for his expectations and negotiations with clients, he felt liberated (Circle). As someone with a strong preference for Circle, he can now explain his creative and emotional needs to people who see things through the Square. He feels empowered to recognize and protect his boundaries, whether personal or professional.

Lesson Learned: In life, the Square is generally dominant... yet it is ready to be used astutely to liberate and give space to Circle.

Meet Denise

"Circle gives you energy, Square provides structure. You need both. But clearly without energy, structure alone is useless to an entrepreneur."

Nature of the challenge:

Unable to overcome a business break-up.

Situation:

A successful entrepreneur, Denise felt everything that she had worked for in the past twenty-five years was about to be stolen from her.

Context:

An African American self-made fashion entrepreneur, Denise was ending a twenty-five-year business partnership. For the first fifteen years, she and her partner had been married; for the last ten, they had been business partners only. This was a big chapter to close. Together they had built from nothing a multimillion-dollar business with multiple retail stores. Denise knew that she had to leave, but she was facing many legal battles to extricate herself from her company and had no family support.

Process to Breakthrough:

Playing the SQUIRCLE Game made Denise very aware of her body and how to tune into it in a way she had never experienced before. A visual person, she also really connected to SQUIRCLE's graphic representation; it intuitively made sense to her. So, during this intense and difficult time of legal processes and transactions, she made the commitment to listen more closely to her body and her emotions. For example, although she had never taken naps before, she stopped every time she felt that her body needed a rest. This in turn helped her to become more patient and learn the value of time, beyond merely setting and reaching deadlines. She also found that she was better able to step back and reflect on the natural rhythms of life and business and to recognize that this time of uncertainty was a necessary stage in a larger journey. This gave her more confidence in her own strengths and in her innate ability to navigate the many obstacles and emotional challenges of her business breakup. In her own words, it turned her downward spiral into a virtuous circle that prevented her from sinking into depression at a time when she needed to be positive, proactive, and on her game. Slowly but surely, she was able to let go of harsh feelings of loss and hurt, and set aside unresolved conflicts in order to move forward.

Outcome:

Denise will tell you that SQUIRCLE saved her from having a nervous breakdown. It was that extreme and that beneficial. She was able to free herself from the past and begin to envision her next entrepreneurial venture. She now recognizes Circle and Square approaches in others and is using SQUIRCLE to help her hire, communicate and collaborate with, and lead employees at her new start-up.

Lesson Learned: A new awareness of her creative self (Circle) applied to concrete business and legal situations (Square) helped her to reconcile her need to leave the business with her fear of the unknown.

Meet Diego

"SQUIRCLE is a process, a journey. It's something you need to learn over and over again. The more you practice, the better you get at it, and the more energized you become."

Nature of the Challenge:

How to motivate people in a government agency.

Situation:

Diego needed to motivate a group of government workers who saw no benefit in making changes.

Context:

Diego is a Dominican American who works in a midsize city on the West Coast as a government officer. He found it hard to inspire his colleagues to get on board with projects that he felt would make a difference for the agency and the community. Employees in his office tended to stick with their routine and what they knew. They did not believe that there was a real incentive to change.

Process to Breakthrough:

One of the ways in which SQUIRCLE most impacted Diego was in showing him how much more he could accomplish when he connected with others on a deeper level than when he was simply functioning on his own. He explains that it is "more than just the energy of the group that you find yourself in. It's the energy that is revealed by being in a group in a certain way, where individuals are fully connected with themselves but no longer about themselves only. This became obvious to me when playing the SQUIRCLE Game, and I saw how I could implement it in the office." At work, he shifted from perceiving himself as alone (Square) to seeing himself as part of a much larger whole (Circle). He stopped trying to convince people of his ideas. Instead, he would engage the group differently, trusting the integrity of where he was coming from but accepting that he couldn't control the outcome. This made him highly receptive to the group's process, which in turn opened him up to new interactions with others and enabled a renewed sense of possibility to emerge among the members of the group. It also gave Diego more energy and more patience; if a plan didn't work the first time, he would try a second time. Eventually his efforts would yield results or he would decide to engage with different people.

Outcome:

He found himself surprisingly more creative, more understanding, and more capable of motivating others to tap into their full potential. He was able to not only handle his colleagues differently but ultimately get them to develop a couple of interesting projects that were important to Diego.

Lesson Learned: Diego discovered how to be in the flow with others and how to positively influence team dynamics and reap concrete outcomes at work.

Meet Bora

"SQUIRCLE is an image; it's a tool; it's a presence. It's the path to make the impossible possible. Once you get it, you simply need to hold the image present in your mind and dear to your heart."

Nature of the Challenge:

To embrace and express her full self.

Situation:

In spite of her huge success as a financial adviser, Bora felt something was not right with her life.

Context:

Bora, a Korean American, appeared to have a perfect life. She is a successful and impactful financial adviser. She runs her own business under a global financial brand. She is the sun of her solar system, the forever provider to all those around her, including her family. But she is running a low-grade grudge against her success.

Process to Breakthrough:

As soon as she was introduced to the Square and the Circle, Bora saw her life and herself differently. SQUIRCLE helped her to recognize that she is inherently, organically a Circle, but that life's circumstances and her career had mutated her into a Square. Once she understood this, she was able to fully realize and acknowledge that she had taken on and adjusted to a role that was not naturally her. She decided to immediately act on this insight and revisit her professional and personal choices.

Outcome:

All of Bora's relationships shifted. First and foremost was her relationship with herself. To embrace her Circle, she joined a stand-up comedy class "just for fun." She didn't think she would find the time to attend twice a week, but she did! The goal of the class was to put together a show and perform in front of an audience. Again, she told herself that she'd do the class when she could but wouldn't showcase anything. Nevertheless, she kept seeing possibilities in the corner of her eye (Circle), which glimmered as a positive reinforcement that it was OK to leave her options open. She persisted (Square) in spite of what seemed truly impossible at times considering her three children, her consuming job responsibilities, caregiving for her ailing father, and her other leadership role at a global nonprofit. She ultimately performed a showcase set and received a standing ovation! As she found more balance, her grudge dissolved and her transformation brought joy into her family life, her career, and most importantly, to herself.

Lesson learned: Bora gave herself permission to have fun, and allowed her Circle to emerge from within her Square persona and become visible to the world.

QUESTIONS

- After reading SQUIRCLE and doing the exercises, what has changed in terms of how you think about your relationships, your work, and your personal life?
- How might you describe your SQUIRCLE experience to colleagues? To friends?

conclusion

In so far as theories of mathematics speak about reality, they are not certain, and in so far as they are certain, they do not speak about reality.

— ALBERT EINSTEIN

What you do makes a difference, and you have to decide what kind of difference you want to make.

— JANE GOODALL

A s we near the end of this book, I hope that you now see the immense opportunity that we all have to adapt and thrive in today's world, and to create a better and sustainable future together, one decision at a time.

We can transition toward a novel way of living in sync with nature. It might seem like a lofty goal, but it is fundamentally possible. From Virginie who was born deaf yet mastered communication to become a lawyer, to Philipp who ran his best marathon ever without a strategy or plan, to our SQUIRCLE atelier participants who made the impossible possible in their lives, these spirited people all point to the same conclusion: anyone can do it. All it takes is a change of attitude. Yes, a radical one, but nothing else.

Some historians believe that around twelve thousand years ago, we shifted from hunting and fishing as a means of gathering food to exploiting the earth's soils through farming. This may have been the decisive moment in which we thought that we had found a more secure and fruitful way to live. We attempted to turn nature into what it's not: a predictable machine. But if this is true, we need to have empathy for mankind and patience with our own transformation. It's hard enough for us to change our personal habits. Imagine what we're up against: trying to evolve beyond millennia-old myths, beliefs, institutions, systems, and organizations.

As daunting as this might be, with a renewed awareness and the right framework, we can begin to understand that omnipotence is a dangerous illusion and vulnerability is the ultimate strength. As we honor the wisdom of our bodies and learn to more shrewdly use the power of science, we can reinvent the way we think and usher in a new path to prosperity.

Can we trust that a humble, reverent respect for the great mystery of nature is every bit as valuable as our intellectual quest to understand it? Is there a way for us to be happy and prosper as a civilization without knowing all the answers and wanting to achieve, above all else, control? SQUIRCLE is here to help us all with these questions. It is my greatest hope that it will help you as it helped me and thousands of others create a new road for yourself with confidence and enthusiasm, and a legacy for many generations to come.

Now is the time for you to take action!

Here is to you, SQUIRCLE reader!

Our SQUIRCLE ADAPTATION course FOR FREE.

It is specifically designed to apply the techniques, tools, and tips presented in the book to embrace your natural ability to thrive in uncertainty.

https://www.squircleacademy.com/squircle-adaptation

You can also contact us to book a conference or seminar, purchase customized copies in bulk for your employees, or hire our consulting services.

Finally, you can follow our charitable initiatives to accelerate gender equality with SQUIRCLE programs, in a way fully inclusive of men.

https://www.knowbetterworldfoundation.org

bibliography

Bailey, Chris. *Hyperfocus: How to Be More Productive in a World of Distraction*. New York: Viking, 2018.

Bolte Taylor, Jill. *My Stroke of Insight: A Brain Scientist's Personal Journey*. Penguin Books, 2008.

Brown, Stuart. *Play. How It Shapes the Brain, Opens the Imagination, and Invigorates the Soul*. Avery, Reprint Edition, 2010.

Damásio, António. *Self Comes to Mind: Constructing the Conscious Brain*. New York: Pantheon Books, 2010.

Doidge, Norman. *The Brain That Changes Itself: Stories of Personal Triumph from the Frontiers of Brain Science*. New York: Viking, 2007.

Gerzeman, John, and Michael D'Antonio. *The Athena Doctrine: How Women (and the Men Who Think Like Them) Will Rule the Future*. San Francisco: Jossey-Bass, 2013.

Gigerenzer, Gerd. *Gut Feelings: The Intelligence of the Unconscious*. Penguin Books, 2007.

Gigerenzer, Gerd. *Risk Savvy: How to Make Good Decisions*. Penguin Books, 2015.

Gopnik, Alison. *The Gardener and the Carpenter: What the New Science of Child Development Tells Us About the Relationship Between Parents and Children.* New York: Farrar, Straus and Giroux, 2016.

Jung, Carl. *Psychological Types.* Trans. H. G. Baynes. Eastford, CT: Martino Fine Books, 2016. First published 1921 by Rascher Verlag (Zurich).

Laloux, Frederic. *Reinventing Organizations: A Guide to Creating Organizations Inspired by the Next Stage of Human Consciousness.* Millis, MA: Nelson Parker, 2014.

Leonard, George. *The Silent Pulse.* New York: Plume, 1986. First published 1977 by Gibbs Smith (Layton, UT).

Mandela, Nelson. *Long Walk to Freedom.* Randburg, South Africa: Macdonald Purnell, 1994.

Steel, Piers. *The Procrastination Equation: How to Stop Putting Things Off and Start Getting Stuff Done.* New York: HarperCollins, 2010.

Weinberg, Gabriel, and Lauren McCann. *Super Thinking: The Big Book of Mental Models.* New York: Portfolio, 2019.

notes

Author's Note

1. Einstein to Eduard Study, September 25, 1918, in the Einstein Archive, Hebrew University, Jerusalem; trans. D. Howard, *Perspectives on Science* 1 (1993), 225.

2. Dr. Jane Goodall, "Nous sommes arrivés à un tournant décisif de notre relation avec le monde naturel," *Good Planet*, May 4, 2020. https://www.goodplanet.info/2020/05/04/dr-jane-goodall-nous-sommes-arrives-a-un-tournant-decisif-dans-notre-relation-avec-le-monde-naturel/?utm_source=mailpoet&utm_medium=email&utm_campaign=selection-hebdomadaire-goodplanet-mag_9

Introduction

1. Albert Einstein, "Principles of Research" (address for Max Planck's sixtieth birthday, Physical Society, Berlin, 1918).

2. António Damásio, *New York Times*, July 28, 2009, https://www.nytimes.com/2009/07/28/health/research/28brain.html.

3. Gerd Gigerenzer, *Risk Savvy: How To Make Good Decisions*, Penguin Books, 2015.

4. Marcus Noland and Tyler Moran, "Study: Firms with More Women in the C-Suite Are More Profitable," *Harvard Business Review*, February 8, 2016, https://hbr.org/2016/02/study-firms-with-more-women-in-the-c-suite-are-more-profitable.

5. Chris Bart and Gregory McQueen, "Why Women Make Better Directors," *International Journal of Business Governance and Ethics* 8, no. 1 (2013): 93-99, https://dx.doi.org/10.1504/IJBGE.2013.052743.

6. Cassie Werber, "Melinda Gates' 'Equality Can't Wait' campaign wants to eliminate the gender pay gap." *World Economic Forum in collaboration with Quartz,* August 21, 2019. https://www.weforum.org/agenda/2019/08/women-walk-bar-208-years-later-paid-same-men/

Chapter 1

1. Unspecified author. "Understanding the Stress Response," *Harvard Health Publishing,* Harvard Medical School, May 1, 2018.

Chapter 2

1. Henri Poincaré, *Science and Method,* Dover Publications,1918.

Chapter 3

1. Ole Henrik Magga, "Diversity in Saami Terminology for Reindeer, Snow, and Ice," *International Social Science Journal* 58, no. 187 (2006): 25-34, https://doi.org/10.1111/j.1468-2451.2006.00594.x.

2. António Damásio, *Self Comes to Mind: Constructing the Conscious Brain* (New York: Pantheon Books, 2010).

3. Sophie Kleber, "3 Ways AI is Getting More Emotional," *Harvard Business Review,* July 31, 2018, https://hbr.org/2018/07/3-ways-ai-is-getting-more-emotional.

Chapter 4

1. Nelson Mandela, *Long Walk to Freedom* (Randburg, South Africa: Macdonald Purnell, 1994).

Chapter 5

1. https://www.aljazeera.com/ajimpact/cleaning-germany-reaches-deal-shut-coal-plants-200116080124654.html.

2. Bo E Madsen and Povl Krogsgaard, "Offshore Wind Power 2010," archived June 30, 2011, at the Wayback Machine. BTM Consult, November 22, 2010.

3. Global Wind Energy Council, *Global Wind Report 2018,* April 2019, https://gwec.net/wp-content/uploads/2019/04/GWEC-Global-Wind-Report-2018.pdf.

4. Sarah Young, "The Real Cost of Your Clothes: These Are the Fabrics with the Best and Worst Environmental Impact," *The Independent*, August 19, 2019, https://www.independent.co.uk/life-style/fashion/fabrics-environment-fast-fashion-eco-friendly-pollution-waste-polyester-cotton-fur-recycle-a8963921.html.

5. Vanessa Friedman, "The Biggest Fake News in Fashion," *New York Times*, December 20, 2018, https://www.nytimes.com/2018/12/18/fashion/fashion-second-biggest-polluter-fake-news.html.

6. Ibid.

7. Adele Peters, "This New H&M Dress Is Made from Wood and Recycled Jeans," *Fast Company*, February 3, 2020, https://www.fastcompany.com/90458767/this-new-hm-dress-is-made-from-wood-and-recycled-jeans.

8. Wageningen University and Research Center, "Agriculture is the direct driver for worldwide deforestation," *Science Daily*, September 25, 2012.

9. Andre Leu, "Organic Agriculture Can Feed the World" *Regeneration International*, October 22, 2018, https://regenerationinternational.org/2018/10/22/organic-agriculture-can-feed-the-world/

10. *Environmental Research Letters* 12, no. 3 (Bristol, UK: IOP Science, 2017), https://iopscience.iop.org/issue/1748-9326/12/3.

11. Gangwei Pan, Helan Xu, Bingnan Mu, Bomou Ma, Jing Yang, Yiqi Yang. Complete stereo-complexation of enantiomeric polylactides for scalable continuous production. *Chemical Engineering Journal*, 2017; 328: 759 DOI: 10.1016/j.cej.2017.07.068

12. *Victim of the Brain*, directed by Piet Hoenderdos (Netherlands: 1988), docudrama, 90 min. A docudrama about the ideas of Douglas Hofstadter.

13. M. Mitchell Waldrop, "The Trillion-Dollar Vision of Dee Hock," *Fast Company*, October 31, 1996.

14. https://www.grameenamerica.org/impact

Chapter 6

1. Alejandro Pérez, Manuel Carreiras, and Jon Andoni Duñabeitia, "Brain-to-Brain Entrainment: EEG Interbrain Synchronization While Speaking and Listening," *Scientific Reports* 7 (2017), https://doi.org/10.1038/s41598-017-04464-4.

2. Sarah W Lazar et al., "Meditation Experience is Associated With In-

creased Cortical Thickness," US National Library of Medicine, National Institutes of Health, November 28, 2005.

3. Alvin Powell, "When Science Meets Mindfulness," *Harvard Gazette Health & Medicine*, April 9, 2018.

4. Katherine Reynolds Lewis, "Abandon Parenting, and Just Be a Parent," *The Atlantic*, September 23, 2016, https://www.theatlantic.com/family/archive/2016/09/abandon-parenting-and-just-be-a-parent/501236/.

5. Norman Doidge, *The Brain that Changes Itself: Stories of Personal Triumph from the Frontiers of Brain Science* (New York: Viking, 2007).

Chapter 8

1. Anne Feyerherm and Cheryl Rice, "Emotional Intelligence and Team Performance: The Good, the Bad and the Ugly," *International Journal of Organization Analysis* 10, no. 4 (2002), 343-362, https://www.researchgate.net/deref/http%3A%2F%2Fdx.doi.org%2F10.1108%2Feb028957.

2. Stuart Brown, *Play. How It Shapes the Brain, Opens the Imagination, and Invigorates the Soul*, Avery, Reprint Edition, 2010.

3. Darryl Edwards, "Game-Changers: Connecting Physical Activity and Health" (presentation at Move Congress, Hungary, 2019).

4. Stuart Brown, "Play Is More than Just Fun" (presentation at TED Serious Play, Pasadena, California, 2008).

5. At 2019 Move Congress conference.

6. https://ohmy.disney.com/movies/2014/10/30/9-of-the-coolest-things-on-the-pixar-campus/

7. https://www.jmkac.org/arts-industry-program.html   https://www.kohlercompany.com/social-impact/arts/

8. Emily Anthes, "Six Ways to Boost Brain Power," *Scientific American Mind*, February 2009, https://www.scientificamerican.com/article/six-ways-to-boost-brainpower/.

9. P. Iannello et al., "Ambiguity and Uncertainty Tolerance, Need for Cognition, and Their Association with Stress. A Study Among Italian Practicing Physicians," *Medical Education Online* 22, no. 1 (2017), doi: 10.1080/10872981.2016.1270009.

10. J. F. Boswell et al., "Intolerance of Uncertainty: A Common Factor in the Treatment of Emotional Disorders," *Journal of Clinical Psychology* 69, no. 6 (2013), 630-645, doi: 10.1002/jclp.21965.

11. Dan Lovallo and Olivier Sibony, "A Language to Discuss Biases," *McKinsey Quarterly*, March 2010.

12. Dan Lovallo and Olivier Sibony, "The Case for Behavioral Strategy," *McKinsey Quarterly*, March 2010, https://www.mckinsey.com/business-functions/strategy-and-corporate-finance/our-insights/the-case-for-behavioral-strategy.

13. Daniel Kahneman, Dan Lovallo, and Olivier Sibony, "The Big Idea: Before You Make That Big Decision . . .," *Harvard Business Review*, June 2011, https://hbr.org/2011/06/the-big-idea-before-you-make-that-big-decision.

14. N. Kamarulzaman et al., "An Overview of the Influence of Physical Office Environments Towards Employees," *Procedia Engineering* 20 (2011), 262-268, doi: 10.1016/j.proeng.2011.11.164.

15. David Sturt and Todd Nordstrom, "Four Reasons Why Asking for Help Makes You a Stronger, Not Weaker, Leader," *Forbes*, November 1, 2017, https://www.forbes.com/sites/davidsturt/2017/11/01/4-reasons-why-asking-for-help-makes-you-a-stronger-not-weaker-leader/#2c9ae04f3c1a.

16. Ibid.

Chapter 9

1. Andrés Rodríguez-Pose and Viola von Berlepsch, "Population Diversity as a Crucial Source of Long-Term Prosperity in the US," Center for Economic Policy Research, November 10, 2017, https://voxeu.org/article/population-diversity-and-long-term-prosperity.

2. Roger C. Mayer, Richard S. Warr, Jing Zhao, "Do Pro-Diversity Policies Improve Corporate Innovation?" *Financial Management* 47, December 18, 2017. https://doi.org/10.1111/fima.12205

3. Patti Anklam, *Net Work: A Practical Guide to Creating and Sustaining Networks at Work and in the World* (Washington, DC: Society for Neuroscience, 2007).

4. Carl Jung, *Psychological Types*, trans. H. G. Baynes (Eastford, CT: Martino Fine Books, 2016).

Chapter 10

1. Gill Cassar and Dominik Breitinger, "What Causes Us to Burnout at Work?" World Economic Forum, October 10, 2019, https://www.weforum.org/agenda/2019/10/burnout-mental-health-pandemic/.

2. Michael Chui et al., "The Social Economy: Unlocking Value and Productivity Through Social Technologies," McKinsey Global Institute, July 2012, https://www.mckinsey.com/industries/technology-media-and-telecommunications/our-insights/the-social-economy.

3. Adobe, "Email Usage—Working-Age Knowledge Workers (US Trended Results)," August 2019.

4. Matt Plummer, "How to Spend Way Less Time on Email Every Day," *Harvard Business Review*, January 22, 2019, https://hbr.org/2019/01/how-to-spend-way-less-time-on-email-every-day.

5. Ibid.

6. Piers Steel, *The Procrastination Equation: How to Stop Putting Things Off and Start Getting Stuff Done* (New York: HarperCollins, 2010).

7. Chris Bailey, *Hyperfocus: How to Be More Productive in a World of Distraction* (New York: Viking, 2018).

8. Chris Bailey, "Five Research-Based Strategies for Overcoming Procrastination," *Harvard Business Review*, October 4, 2017, https://hbr.org/2017/10/5-research-based-strategies-for-overcoming-procrastination.

acknowledgments

The idea for this book was born years ago after awarded author, former client, and friend Deborah Burns contacted me to discuss and eventually collaborate on an inspiring project about women of significance at a time when women were denied rights and access. I am grateful to her and the many realizations and inspiration this fruitful collaboration brought forth. I am also grateful to senior editor Ann Campbell, who skillfully and relentlessly challenged every idea and sentence that needed to be challenged in the manuscript I handed to her. My special thanks go to senior publishing consultant Folco Chevallier, who advised me every step of the way to the book you're reading, editor Jessica Hatch for her scrupulous final review of the manuscript, and Heather Holley for lending her fine voice to SQUIRCLE audiobook. I also would like to wholeheartedly thank a very wise woman and very dear friend Dominique Dubois for constantly stimulating and inspiring new insights and perspectives that enriched this book and that keep enriching my work and my life in so many ways. I also thank all other thinkers, authors, and creative minds who preceded this book and offered a wealth of creative ideas; I tried to give justice to their work in quoting my sources, but of course they are not exhaustive. In this respect, I would like to acknowledge Mark Kuras, PhD, and the work I was privileged to do with him in New York; Tiokasin Ghosthorse and the tradition and wisdom of his venerable elders; and professional partner in crime and friend Christine Hauri, who assisted me in this work and provided support as much as she brought creative genius, talent, and skills to the table. Many thanks to all my colleagues at The Human Company for their multiple contributions, and to clients around the world who allowed me to develop further and put to the test the ideas presented in this book. Grateful thanks also to corporate supporters and early adopters Guillaume de Lesquen at Ralph Lauren, Hugues de Pins at Cartier, John Loughlin at Apple News, Sharon Jacquet at JP Morgan Chase, and especially to Sonja Winther at Chantelle. Finally, a warm thank-you to early readers; SQUIRCLE atelier participants, especially Bernard, Bridget, David, Debi, Florence, Michele B., Michele M., Rebecka, and Ron; and all other supporters for joining and encouraging me in the early stages of the SQUIRCLE book development; the help that each one of them provided was so useful and is greatly appreciated.

I feel privileged to conclude this section of the book with the thankful mention of a serendipitous gift—which unexpectedly led to the invention of Square and Circle—from long-time supporter and dear friend Mercedes Erra, advertising entrepreneur extraordinaire, a woman of exception, mother of five and leader of an ingenious tribe of almost a thousand employees in Paris.

about the author

A global leader in creating social innovation for a sustainable future, Francis Cholle has worked with some of the largest and most successful companies in the world, including Apple, Bouygues, Bristol Myers Squibb, Citigroup, Danone, Estée Lauder, Hachette, Johnson & Johnson, JP Morgan Chase, L'Oréal, Shiseido, Total, and Veolia. Empowering CEOs with new ways to create sustainable value, Francis's core mission focuses on unleashing untapped potential key to achieving a competitive advantage: intuitive intelligence. As founder and CEO of The Human Company, Francis employs a holistic approach to drive improvements in human performance and acceleration in business transformation. His proprietary methodology, based on his awarded, science-based model, The Intuitive Compass®, and his leadership mindset of the future, Intuitive Intelligence Know Better™, was featured in media like the Wall Street Journal, BFM TV, and TechCrunch TV, as well as presented at the Davos World Economic Forum and on the TED stage.

With The Human Company, Francis has engaged notable clients to transform their organizations. Retained by Ralph

Lauren, Francis worked directly with the company's global president to reinvent a declining product line, effectively taking it from a capitalized annual growth rate (CAGR) of negative 24 percent to a CAGR of plus 10 percent in a single year and doubling global market growth over five consecutive years. In another engagement with Lagardère Sports and Entertainment, Francis employed his methodology and approach to reinvent and redefine the company's business model. With Francis's strategic guidance, the company's entity in Europe, the Middle East, and Africa (EMEA), which had been operating at a loss, returned to profitability within twelve months.

Francis's purpose when founding The Human Company was to demonstrate to himself and to global leaders his creative vision of the path to sustainable prosperity. He has proved across continents and industries that reconnecting with our gut instinct, the intelligence of nature within, is a necessary step to resolve our global challenges. Without fail, this process both liberates unprecedented levels of creativity, agility, and business performance and can facilitate the mandatory cultural shift from an exploitative to a regenerative relationship with nature. After fifteen years of successful C-level advisory work, Francis developed the SQUIRCLE Academy, an educational platform to create systemic change on a global scale by teaching a new brand of leadership to individuals across generations. In addition, he launched the Know Better World Foundation to empower women to become the entrepreneurs of their lives, the proven fastest track to our return to a sustainable and prosperous model of development.

Francis is about to impart this "new way of thinking for a new world" to a larger global audience with his upcoming philosophical tale and animated movie, both based on the life of an unusual king who made history saving his people from famine, thanks to his visionary wife and daughter.

Francis is a contributor to numerous global business publications. As a bestselling published author, his books are available in multiple languages, including English, French, Mandarin, and Portuguese. Francis is on the faculty of the School of Visual Arts in New York. He regularly lectures at top graduate business schools worldwide, such as the Wharton School at the University of Pennsylvania, Columbia University, New York University Stern School of Business, the Fashion Institute of Technology, and at the HEC MBA in Paris, France.

Francis holds both bachelor's and master's degrees from Europe's leading business school, the HEC School of Management in Paris, as well as a diploma in clinical psychology from the Tomatis Center in Paris. He is also a trained actor, director, classical singer, and a certified yogi. A dual French-US citizen, he lives in Los Angeles, CA.

CPSIA information can be obtained
at www.ICGtesting.com
Printed in the USA
LVHW091517160920
666190LV00014B/163

9 781735 138435